D1536653

Spiritual Counsel
in the Anglican Tradition

Spiritual Counsel
in the Anglican Tradition

DAVID HEIN

AND

CHARLES R. HENERY

EDITORS

WIPF & STOCK · Eugene, Oregon

SPIRITUAL COUNSEL IN THE ANGLICAN TRADITION

Wipf & Stock
An Imprint of Wipf and Stock Publishers
199 W. 8th Ave., Suite 3
Eugene, OR 97401
www.wipfandstock.com

ISBN 13: 978-1-55635-419-9

Manufactured in the U.S.A.

Cover photograph of St. Paul's Cathedral, London, January 1942, courtesy of the Imperial War Museum. The destruction caused by Nazi air attacks is softened by a dusting of snow.

Contents

Foreword

"THE DEEPEST SIGNIFICANCE OF the past," writes the former archbishop of Canterbury Michael Ramsey, "is that it contains reflections of what is eternal. Saintly men and women of any age belong to more than their own era: they transcend it." In *Spiritual Counsel in the Anglican Tradition*, David Hein and Charles Henery not only present this insight of Archbishop Ramsey's (in the chapter "A Pilgrim's Journey"); they also demonstrate its truth through the whole scope of their anthology. Saints necessarily exemplify their own time and culture, yet somehow they also stretch beyond these limits, living as they do on the eschatological edge of the kingdom. When holy men and women leave us some tangible part of their thought and prayer through their writings, our sense of the communion of saints is immensely deepened. The living and the dead meet as contemporaries, addressing one another across centuries.

Sometimes we find that part of the benefit in reading earlier authors lies in their very distance from us. Samuel Johnson could be none other than an eighteenth-century thinker, while John Donne reflects the English Renaissance at its best. And so the various Anglican authors contained in this volume, spanning four centuries and two continents, will challenge our characteristic assumptions simply by being people of their own times and places—gifted people, to be sure, but still products of their distinct historical contexts. After reading them, we may find we want to consider cultivating virtues admired in a previous era, but now out of fashion; these virtues may still be needful for us. Our horizons can be enlarged by fellow pilgrims whose outlook on God, on life, or on the Church is not quite our own, pressing us to examine our own perspectives afresh.

Every generation seeks some embodiment of the "wonderful counselor" Isaiah extolled. And in every generation, the grace of holy Wisdom resides in faithful Christians of exceptional discernment. Here "the reflections of what is eternal" may show up as counsel that is consistently apposite. While books cannot entirely substitute for personal guidance, they can help steer us through the sometimes rough and confusing terrain of the soul when access to face-to-face pastoral care may be limited by geography or other circumstances. Even when we enjoy sound mentoring, these authors continue to educate us in the ways of the Spirit. *Spiritual Counsel in the Anglican Tradition* draws upon sage representatives of the Anglican family, some of whom are well-known figures, while others are more obscure.

As we become more acquainted with them, we will probably wish to delve into the writings of those who address us most helpfully and pointedly; and if we are driven back to the sources, this collection of diverse writings will have been all the more successful in its pastoral goal. The topical—not chronological—grouping of these selections underscores our solidarity with every generation that aspires to maturity in Christ, and it assists the reader who wishes to pursue a particular avenue of thought. As in a good conversation, words need to be punctuated by thoughtful silence. I suggest using these texts as a form of *lectio divina*, reading no more than a selection or two a day, meditating on them, pondering their practical application, and finally allowing them to serve as a springboard for prayer.

The sections that deal with our corporate sacramental life, the mystery of Christ experienced through the round of the church year, and aspects of personal prayer all strengthen these essential foundations of Christian discipleship. Yet Anglican pastoral thinking has never focused exclusively on worship and prayer as the sole domain of the Spirit. On the contrary, Anglican spirituality characteristically seeks a robust sanctification of the ordinary, "so that God may be glorified in all things" (1 Pet 4:11). Hence we find the Anglican counselors in these pages concerned with such mundane matters as friendship, the care of children, marriage, money, work, art, aging, animals, and the created order. Nothing in our lives is to be untouched by grace. We need the integrative wisdom of these Anglican forebears to see how, even in the microcosm of our lives, in Christ "all things hold together" (Col 1:17).

Julia Gatta

The School of Theology at the University of the South

Sewanee, Tennessee

Preface

THE STREAM OF SPIRITUAL conversation that flows in these pages represents the confluence of three tributaries. First, almost twenty years ago, there was my little collection *Readings in Anglican Spirituality*, which Forward Movement Publications brought out in 1991. Professors may sneer at mass-market trade publishers and eschew get-rich-quick publishing schemes, but they are secretly pleased when their books appear in hundreds of academic libraries.

Readings made it into about the same number of institutional libraries as the total number of fingers that I have on my two hands. Nevertheless, the general response was gratifying because that slim paperback appeared to connect with the audience it was specifically aimed at: harried, frequently confused Christians or would-be Christians in search of spiritual knowledge and guidance. The first book I had worked on which tried to reach a non-academic audience of ordinary Christians, *Readings* was read and appreciated—I was pleased to hear—by enough people to make me feel that this departure from the accustomed path of scholarly publication had been worthwhile. Ever since, I have regularly tried to address both professional and lay audiences.

Inspired to continue tapping this rich vein of Anglican literature, I came across additional material from the past four centuries which looked as if it too might nourish the hearts, minds, and souls of hungry Christians. Some outstanding passages were found in places where a reader would expect to come upon great advice in fine language, such as the essays of the brilliant conversationalist and man of letters Samuel Johnson. But other good material was discovered in places where an informed, perhaps jaded, Anglican would never expect to encounter wise thoughts in powerful prose: the annual convention addresses of bishops of the Episcopal Church. Starting in the 1940s, the Right Reverend Noble Cilley Powell regularly gave his people in the diocese of Maryland reasons to listen to what he had to say.

This valuable new material found its way into a series—"Spiritual Counsel in the Anglican Tradition"—that I edited for the *Anglican Theological Review* in the 1990s. Published with the hearty encouragement of the journal's editor-in-chief, the theologian Jim Griffiss, this series is also largely represented in the pages that follow.

In the meantime, other collections of Anglican spiritual writings have appeared. Perhaps the best—at least the one that I turn to most often—is Richard H. Schmidt's *Glorious Companions: Five Centuries of Anglican Spirituality* (Eerdmans, 2002). One reason for producing such books is the desire to deepen the spirituality of those who are already within the Church. But undoubtedly another reason is the wish to make it clear to twenty-first-century readers that a viable alternative to "I'm spiritual but not religious" does exist: "I'm spiritual in the original meaning of 'spiritual'—spiritual within a long religious tradition and within a specific religious community."

The editors of collections such as Schmidt's are explicitly addressing Christians and implicitly addressing readers who are "spiritual but not religious." They seem to be saying to the latter: "Here in this book is evidence to provoke you to rethink both the foundation and the form of your spirituality." Valuable as these recent collections of spiritual writings are, however, they are not exactly what *Readings in Anglican Spirituality* and this book promise to be: collections that specialize in spiritual counsel.

Believing, therefore, that a need continued to exist for a body of extracts that speak directly to the reader, offering to him or her useful words of instruction and guidance, I called upon a friend of twenty years' standing to join me as coeditor of a revised and expanded collection. Even after raiding *Readings* and culling from the best of the *ATR* series, I realized that more good material was needed to make a book.

Having recently stepped down after twenty-five years at Nashotah House, a historic Episcopal seminary in Wisconsin, the Reverend Dr. Charles Henery, I knew, could summon the knowledge and apply the fine judgment necessary to help give this project the completion it called for. At Nashotah, he was both the William Schaff Helmuth Professor of Ecclesiastical History and the John Maury Allin Distinguished Professor of Homiletics. Father Henery, who now serves as Director of Spiritual Life at St. John's Northwestern Military Academy, in Delafield, Wisconsin, has found, selected, and edited many valuable new pieces relating to the pilgrim's journey: from birth (baptism) to death (spiritual, physical)—and beyond (heaven). I am tremendously grateful to him for his outstanding contribution not only to the quantity but also to the quality of the readings in this book. He has been an excellent partner in this enterprise, and, in all truth, without him this book would never have seen the light of day.

David Hein

Frederick, Maryland
Christmas 2009

Acknowledgments

W E, THE EDITORS, WISH to thank Jennifer Henery, a PhD candidate in theology at Marquette University, for her assistance in a number of areas. We especially appreciate her skills in the science of information technology and her talents in the art of dealing with publishers to secure permissions at the lowest possible cost.

In addition, William Lane, copyeditor, pulled this manuscript together, put the text in the correct format, and cast a sharp editorial eye over all the contents. We are grateful to him for all his professional abilities, but especially for his cheerful manner and persevering nature.

Aimee Gil, interlibrary loan librarian at Hood College, was both efficient and proficient in completing her tasks. We thank her not only for her timely assistance but also for her good humor and resourceful intelligence, displayed over many months.

We owe a special debt of thanks to Julia Gatta, associate professor of pastoral theology in the School of Theology at the University of the South (Sewanee), for providing a vibrant welcome to readers in her foreword to *Spiritual Counsel in the Anglican Tradition*. We are deeply grateful to her for these well-chosen words.

Grateful acknowledgment is also made to the following publishers for permission to use copyright material:

Eerdmans: Excerpts from Donald Coggan, *Convictions*, © 1975, Wm. B. Eerdmans Publishing Co., Grand Rapids, MI. Reprinted by permission of the publisher; all rights reserved. Excerpts from Austin Farrer, *The End of Man*, © 1973, Wm. B. Eerdmans Publishing Co., Grand Rapids, MI. Reprinted by permission of the publisher; all rights reserved. Excerpts from *Glory Descending: Michael Ramsey and His Writings*, © 2005, Wm. B. Eerdmans Publishing Co., Grand Rapids, MI. Reprinted by permission of the publisher; all rights reserved.

Forward Movement: Excerpts from Stephen Bayne, *Now Is the Accepted Time,* © 1983. Used with permission of the Forward Movement Publishing Company.

Houghton Mifflin Harcourt: Excerpts from C. S. Lewis, *The Four Loves,* copyright © C. S. Lewis, 1960, renewed 1988 by Arthur Owen Barfield, reprinted by permission of the Houghton Mifflin Harcourt Publishing Company.

Hymns Ancient and Modern Ltd.: Excerpts from John Macquarrie, *Paths in Spirituality,* are copyright © John Macquarrie, SCM Press, 1992, and reproduced by permission of Hymns Ancient & Modern Ltd. Excerpts from Alec Vidler, *Windsor Sermons,* are copyright © Alec Vidler, SCM Press, 1963, and reproduced by permission of Hymns Ancient and Modern Ltd.

Rowan & Littlefield: Excerpts from Austin Farrer, *Austin Farrer: The Essential Sermons,* 1991, are reprinted by permission of the Rowman & Littlefield Publishing Group.

Society for Promoting Christian Knowledge: Excerpt from Austin Farrer, *The Brink of Mystery,* edited by Charles C. Conti. London: SPCK, 1976. Reprinted by permission of the publisher.

Introduction

A S THE WORLD GROWS increasingly complex, human beings need more, not less, good counsel for Christian living. This book reaches into the treasury of Anglican spirituality and draws out pearls of wisdom for today's needs. The Anglican tradition has shown an abiding concern for a holy living that leads to a holy dying. The present work offers earnest, practical devotion to inspire and to instruct the Christian pilgrim in the path of discipleship. Here you will find not a general collection of spiritual writings but direct words of spiritual counsel. Moreover, you will encounter many passages selected for both their authoritative content and their surpassing beauty. This book takes seriously the Anglican emphasis on a form of religion that quickens the mind, forms the conscience, guides the will, and lifts the spirit.

Having said that, we recognize that no book can substitute—in immediacy, vitality, and sensitivity—for a personal relationship. An insightful colleague, a sage spiritual director, or a thoughtful friend will have known you over time, will see you as a distinct individual, and therefore should be able to respond to you in a way that is dynamic rather than static.

Although marks on paper can never replace that kind of encounter, it remains true that the relation between reader and text is not a static one, either, and that the printed word possesses its own unmistakable companionability. Authors in this volume have been friends to generation after generation, they have spoken to all sorts and conditions of men and women, and they retain the capacity to say the fitting thing here and now.

The present collection may not include your favorite writer on spiritual matters. You would certainly be correct to point out that English spirituality comprises a far richer and more variegated set of works than is represented in these pages. It rests upon the Old and New Testaments and the *Book of Common Prayer*; it includes such figures as Anselm of Canterbury, Julian of Norwich, Walter Hilton, Richard Rolle, Margery Kempe, and the author of *The Cloud of Unknowing*—all of whom wrote well before the sixteenth century. But editors have to draw the line somewhere, and so for reasons not entirely arbitrary this book cites only those who are heirs of the Tudor Reformation.

The main purpose of this volume is not to introduce you to some great figures in the history of the Church or to give you a taste of some fine prose, although both of these experiences can be enjoyed along the way. The primary justification for this collection is to allow some compelling voices from the Anglican tradition—a *via media* both fully protestant and fully catholic—to speak directly to you: heart to heart, mind to mind, soul to soul.

We live in an era of pluralism and rapid social change. Ours is a polytheistic age of shifting value centers and shaky commitments. Many times, counselors even within the Church neglect what Professor Don Browning of the University of Chicago Divinity School has spoken of as "the moral context of pastoral care." Employing a method that is basically "eductive," counselors may seek only to support the client as he or she "clarifies" his or her values.[1]

Of course, this therapeutic approach can be extremely helpful. To flee to the opposite extreme is to embrace legalism and moralism, and thus to risk undermining authentic selfhood. We are right to be wary of the tyranny of "the should" and to want to discover our own true paths in life. But we also have to acknowledge that the road we most often travel is not one that cuts through virgin forest but is rather a cluttered and confusing route punctuated by signs and signals of every kind. A person seeking trustworthy counsel is simply asking to be shown a few reliable signposts along the way.

In the Anglican tradition of spiritual reflection, a heavy emphasis has always been placed upon individual responsibility and the use of a person's distinctive powers of thinking and willing. As Stephen Neill has pointed out, "the Anglican appeal is to the intellect, the conscience, and

---

1. Browning, *The Moral Context of Pastoral Care.*

the will." The individual who must decide and choose is not left alone, however, but is sustained by the Body of Christ.[2]

St. Augustine well understood the need that all Christians have of this continuing assistance. In his biography of the bishop of Hippo, Peter Brown observes that the *Confessions* did not give the conventional Christian of sixteen hundred years ago quite what he or she wanted: the book came as a surprise and an annoyance to many. Why? Because it was not what readers expected: the account of a successful conversion. It was not the story of a total transformation simple and dramatic and final.

Augustine's experience of conversion did not mean that he had now arrived safely in port. The author of the *Confessions* makes it clear that the harbor of the convert is still buffeted by storms—or, in another image, that even the baptized Christian must remain an invalid.[3] As Peter Brown writes, "Like the wounded man, found near death by the wayside in the Parable of the Good Samaritan, [Augustine's] life had been saved by the rite of baptism; but he must be content to endure, for the rest of his life, a prolonged and precarious convalescence in the 'Inn' of the Church."[4] The authors of the extracts provided here may be thought of as experienced, well-recommended servants of this Inn.

This minimal orientation should suffice by way of an introduction. Each chapter has an internal structure, of course, as does this book as a whole; but by no means has this volume been arranged so that it needs to be read through from first page to last. Sketching this book's complete program in advance seems, therefore, rather beside the point.

The only injunction that you might consider taking to heart is a fairly obvious one. It has to do not with this book's architecture but with its tempo. Where you begin hardly matters because you should read as your heart moves you and the Spirit leads you. But how you read what you feel inclined to read is a different matter. If this undertaking is truly to become an exercise in spiritual reading, then the proper pace is *lentamente*. If you read slowly, then you may discern meanings that the extracts' authors possibly—and the editors probably—were not aware of: another reason for the editors to forgo trying to foreshadow this work's contents, for how could they say for certain what those contents are?

2. Neill, *Anglicanism*, 423–24.
3. Brown, *Augustine of Hippo*, 177, 365.
4. Brown, *Augustine of Hippo*, 365.

These excerpts' rough delivery from their matrices—torn from their homes, replanted by editor-nurserymen—has freed these words to find new places of habitation. The reader's freedom to discover dovetails with the texts' freedom to signify. What lies on the surface is one thing: a quick perusal takes in nothing worthwhile. Return to the same ground after a heavy rain, when you have more time, and you may descry a half-hidden treasure. A passage that initially puts you off could be found to have something going for it after all. An author whose musty language offends modern sensibilities may nonetheless offer one line in ten or fifteen which speaks to your condition.

Admittedly, in some cases, a writer's approach to a topic—his or her main point—may be readily discernible, his or her meaning both clear and fixed. But, vexed by tone or content, you may simply dislike or disagree with what this author has to say. Thus, instead of gently nudging you toward hearty agreement in some perceived truth, the writer may provoke you into opposition—or into a wider or deeper view than that represented by the extract. The possibility of this achievement in insight on your part is not to be gainsaid: In your disagreement you may well attain to a more profound grasp of the truth—you may proceed farther in the Light—than this supposed expert. In the event, these passages will again have served a useful purpose, for these words are not the last word, set before you as the teaching of a magisterium, defining true doctrine once and for all.

Finally, in all likelihood, you will never find anything worthwhile in some of these texts, either to affirm or to quarrel with. I confess that a few of these excerpts do not connect with me at all, and I have no expectation that they ever will. But others of these passages contain some of the most meaningful and memorable prose I have ever encountered, and I return to these words again and again, year after year.

David Hein

The Love of God

IN FACTS AND IN LEADINGS

What after all are we to say about a Christian acceptance of God's will? Let us say this. God's will is expressed in two ways: in facts and in leadings. Facts express God's will in the sense that they set us our tasks; and the task is very often that we should alter the facts: our sins, for example, or our neighbour's unhappiness. Nothing forces God's will on me more plainly than your unhappiness or than my sin. There is seldom good reason to accept facts as divine dispensations under which we must simply submit. When it comes to dealing with the facts, we look for divine leadings: we have the words and example of Christ, and of his saints; we have our prayers, by which we seek to touch the living movements of God's present creative work. For he is at work in us individually and in our neighbors singly, just as he is in the great movements of mankind. And it is men, after all, it is the souls he makes immortal, that God supremely loves. What shall it profit men to master the universe, if they have hollow hearts? What shall it profit a man to gain the whole world, and lose his own soul?

FARRER, *THE ESSENTIAL SERMONS*, 127–28.

LOVE CRIES TO LOVE

Love ever cries to love, and only in love can love find its rest. When our Lord Jesus Christ drew from St. Peter the threefold profession of love, which was to be set for ever against the threefold denial, He did not ask him for any promise of reformation and virtue. He looked into his soul and simply said, "Lovest thou Me?" He knew perfectly well that if Peter loved Him, out of that love everything would come. Nothing can alter the everlasting love of God for the soul of each one of us, and into whatever mistakes we may be trapped, into whatever sins we may fall, His question is always the same, "Lovest thou Me?" Where the soul can answer, "Lord, Thou knowest all my inconsistency, all my sin, but Thou knowest also that I love Thee," it is on that love He builds.

FATHER ANDREW, *LOVE'S FULFILLMENT*, 141.

SUBLIME IRRELEVANCE

There is a sublime irrelevance in Christ Jesus to what is going on. This is what wins us to Him and frightens us about Him. It is not what helps us to understand Him, because we cannot fit Him into . . . any of our categories. He comes on His own terms. He is God's idea of what it is to be a man, and He is that in His way, the way of the Cross, the way of Love, the way of Passion, the way of Pain, the way of sacrifice, the way of heroism, the way of loneliness, the way of joy, the way of sadness, the way of death, the way of beauty, the way of truth. He abides in His way, and on His terms, and He will not be captured. "This is my beloved Son. Hear Him!" This is where we start and indeed, this is where any deep understanding of the ways of God must start—on God's terms, not ours.

BAYNE, *NOW IS THE ACCEPTED TIME*, 38.

THE LIFE OF WISDOM

In the love of Jesus we find life made sure to us, and the value of life made known to us. All things were created for the glory of God: but man was created to love God, and to behold His glory in Divine fellowship. Faith must keep us from trusting in our own wisdom, which is only ignorance. Hope must lead us to search after Wisdom with diligence, as an abundant recompense for all that may be required of us. Love must teach us to keep the revelations of Divine Wisdom as the strength of our life and our abiding joy amidst a world of change. Whence is the sorrow of the world and its insecurity? It is because the Wisdom of God is no object of faith, or hope, or love to the world. The world understandeth not the things of the Spirit of God, and therefore values them not. But those to whom God has given the spirit of adoption . . . have their understanding enlightened. It is of no use that we are called into this dispensation of spiritual things if we refuse to accept it beyond the judgment of our natural understanding. The search for Wisdom in the life of penitence will leave us the most miserable of all men if we do not keep our eye upon the glory which is in store. But if, while we realize the future glory by hope, we cast ourselves upon the Wisdom of God by faith, we shall indeed find that, hidden though it be, it is a present object of inspiring love, with rich benefactions of grace around the neck, rejoicing the life.

BENSON, *WISDOM*, 119–21.

GOD NOT CRUEL

Never propose to thy self such a God, as thou wert not bound to imitate: Thou mistakest God, if thou make him to be any such thing, or make him to do any such thing, as thou in thy proportion shouldst not be, or shouldst not do. And shouldst thou curse any man that had never offended, never transgrest, never trespast thee? Can God have done so? Imagine God . . . to play but a *game at Chesse* with this world; to sport himself with making little things great, and great things nothing: Imagine God to be but at play with us, but a gamester; yet will a gamester curse, before he be in danger of losing any thing? Will God *curse* man, before man have sinned?

DONNE, *DONNE'S SERMONS*, 140.

INFINITE LOVE

God never wills, nor can will, evil to anyone, anywhere, at any time. God is, has been, and always will be, pure undiluted, unmitigated Beauty, Goodness, and Truth—Infinite Love. Nothing in the world must make you compromise about that. You cannot live, and you cannot think rightly, until you grasp that and hold tight to it. That is the truth which you have to hold by force of faith in the teeth of doubt, steadfastly denying whatever appears to contradict it, denying the world's denial of God's Love.

STUDDERT KENNEDY, *THE WICKET GATE*, 132.

RECEIVING LOVE

The true love of a wife, or child, of a kind friend, or of a gracious benefactor, when it really takes possession of a man, will make a wonderful change in his whole behaviour. It will cause him to deny himself, for the sake of pleasing and profiting those whom he loves: and when once that lesson is learned, there is no saying how greatly a person may improve in a very short time. So it is with a Christian person, if he will give himself up in earnest to the true love of God, when the Holy Spirit has begun to shed it abroad in his heart. It will make all the difference to him in all respects. It will give him faith, for he will set his heart on the things above, which are out of sight, and will order all his ways with a view to them. It will give him courage: he will not mind dangers nor difficulties, so he can please Christ Whom he loves. It will give him knowledge: when we love any one, it makes us quick and sharp in finding out what will please the beloved person. It will give him temperance: ordinary selfish pleasures will be nothing to him, because Christ, Whom he loves, is not in them.

Thus we may in some measure understand, how this one great thing, the Love of God, being truly received into a man's heart, brings with it all other good and holy principles, and makes that possible, nay, easy, which is in itself far beyond all the wisdom and strength of man. The Love of God can do this, because it is, in fact, the Spirit of God moving our hearts; and how can any thing be too hard for the Almighty Spirit of the Most High God?

KEBLE, *SERMONS*, 13.

GOD TELLS US HIS NAME

As God gave Himself a Name, it proves that He is not unknowable, that man can know something, not all, but something about Him. When we are convinced that we can know something of Him, we must trust the amount we cannot know, because that which we do know tells us that God is Love. When two people love one another they are often afraid each of the other, lest the other should find out in them something not so good as they suppose. It is a common experience. But the answer of love is, "I care not—nothing I can discover will affect what you are to me. Love carries all. I know I have your love, and I can rest in that and leave all else." So, in a higher way, of God. . . . I have no fear that what I do not know of Him will contradict what I do know. I do know that God is Love, and that He would not deceive me, so I can trust Him. Thus, brethren, we see He is knowable in part.

And, yet again, by the Name which God gives Himself He teaches us that the definition of Himself cannot be taken from any created thing, but only from Himself. "I AM THAT I AM." He would teach us this, that God is not measurable by any created thing, for He was before all things and was the Creator of all things. So when He tells us His Name,

"I AM THAT I AM," He meant us to learn that He cannot he defined by anything finite, but only by taking the definition from Himself. The words might be translated "I will be what I will be," and it may be to teach us that God is independent of all created things, of space, or matter, and so He is also independent of all time. "I will be what I will be." In that simple word there is much value for us. It teaches us that He is not unknowable, and that for what we do not know we can trust, because we know He is love and love never deceives. We learn too that He cannot be defined by the creature, because He was before all things, and all time. God from everlasting to everlasting.

And yet, if it is so, as we believe, that God is the Creator of all things, why did He rest on the seventh day? From exhaustion, or from a satisfied will? Not from exhaustion, otherwise He is not God. Then, if from a satisfied will, He could have done more? Certainly. He could have made more worlds, or have made the earth bigger, or have made more suns, or stars, or all on a larger scale. He rested from a satisfied will, not from exhaustion. But if God rested from a satisfied will, then it follows that there remains, over and above in God, after the creation of the world, power and wisdom unexpressed.

The attributes of God, and the nature of God were not exhausted. There were power and wisdom over all that He had made.

KING, DUTY AND CONSCIENCE, 82–83.

THE LOVE OF GOD

God so loveth us that He would make all things channels to us and messengers of His love. Do for His sake deeds of love, and He will give thee His love. Still thyself; thy own cares, thy own thoughts, for Him, and He will give thee Himself. Ask for Himself; and He will take thee into Himself. Truly a secret, hidden thing is the love of God, known only to them who seek it, and to them also a secret, for what man can have of it here is, how slight a foretaste of that endless ocean of His love!

PUSEY, SELECTIONS, 7–8.

THE PLEASURES OF OUR LORD

Our Lord Jesus was the one person who was never pleasing Himself. He was never thinking of Himself. He delighted to do His Father's will, and to finish His work. He delighted to think of His Father and of all His infinite love, and of all His purposes of good which He had devised for men, and which He would accomplish for men. Every tree which grew by the watercourse, every flower in the hedgerows, told Him something of his Father's deep, wonderful, careful love; how He had made everything, and lo it was good; how He was watching over everything, to keep it good and beautiful, and bring out the good and beauty of it fully at last. He delighted to think that there was not a publican or sinner despised by man whom His Father did not look after and care for, and seek to bring home to His family. He delighted to think that His Father loved that His children should be healthy, and free, and true. He delighted that his Father had sent Him into the world to give health to the sick, and freedom to those who were in bondage, and to make them good who had been under the power of the evil one. It was meat and drink for Him to work for this end, meat and drink to be sending lepers away well, to be restoring to palsied people the use of their limbs again, to be giving back the dead child alive to its father and mother, the dead man alive to his sisters. He was pleasing His Father in all that He did. He was not seeking His own pleasure in anything. That was joy. If that had been all, Christ's life on earth would have been only one of joy.

MAURICE, *LESSONS OF HOPE*, 57–58.

THE HEART OF LOVE

Amidst the vast scene of the world's problems and tragedies you may feel that your own ministry and witness seems so small, so insignificant, so concerned with the trivial. But consider—the glory of Christianity is its claim that small things really matter, and that the small group, the very few, the one man or woman or child are of infinite worth to God. Let that be your inspiration. Consider our Lord himself. Amidst a vast world with its vast empires and events and tragedies, our Lord devoted himself to a small country, to small things and to individual men and women, often giving hours of time to the few, or to the one man or woman. For the infinite worth of the one person is the key to the Christian understanding of the many. You will never be nearer to Christ than in caring for the one man, the one woman, the one child. His authority will be given to you as you do this, and his joy will be yours as well.

RAMSEY, *GLORY DESCENDING*, 22–23.

2

The Spiritual Life

SPIRITUAL PROGRESS

Progress in the spiritual life, like progress in anything else, requires effort. It requires the systematic and persistent use of means appropriate to the end we are seeking. Indeed the spiritual life is an art, in the successful prosecution of which we require careful training. . . . From time to time, we hear of spiritual geniuses to whom the acquisition of holiness seems to cost little in the way of effort; but to most of us . . . spiritual genius . . . remains a matter of taking pains. We may be glad that this is so, for anyone can take pains.

. . . Curiously, many look to acquire spiritual habits almost over night. They turn from a life of sin or indifference and spiritual inexperience, and do not understand why they do not at once enter into the habits and experience of the saints. But certainly the acquisition of a new center of interest, the withdrawal of the affections from their accustomed objects, the conversion of the will may be expected to take a very considerable time. Spiritual habits are slowly built. We may be satisfied if progress is being made steadily and unswervingly toward our end—the knowledge and love of God.

BARRY, *INVITATIONS*, 1, 22.

A SATISFYING EXPERIENCE

Consider . . . whether you have found in our Lord complete satisfaction of your desires. I do not mean have you wholly attained the accomplishment of your spiritual ambitions; that will never be the case in this life. But while we find the Spiritual Life which results from union with our

Lord and the possession of his Spirit a constantly growing and expanding experience, we also find that it is a satisfying experience. Consciousness of imperfection there must be. Indeed, this paradox is true: The more perfect we grow, the less perfect we seem; seem to ourselves, I mean, because increasing spiritual attainment means increasing insight and increasing severity of judgment. For when we say that the Spiritual Life is a satisfying experience we mean, not that we are increasingly satisfied with self but with our Lord. We find in him the means of satisfying all in our nature that is pure and godlike. And, amid all the stress and strain of our battle with opposing forces—the world, the flesh and the devil—we find the growing experience we have of our Lord translated into interior strength and peace. The battle is severe, but we go to it light hearted as those who are sure of the victory. But this is only on condition of a progressive effort to realize all that union with our Lord means. If the water of the Spirit is to flow from him to us there must be on our side a great eagerness. . . . [A]ll the energy cannot be on the divine side; if there is an energy in giving there must also be an energy in receiving. Passive reception is not enough. We must so receive the energy of the divine life as to transform it into the energy of our own human living. Are you quite sure that that is what is taking place in your experience? The divine offer is made to you: "If any man thirst, let him come" [John 7:37]. Have you come? Have you cared enough to be active? Has the desirability of our Lord overcome the inertia of acquired habit, or the opposition of rooted sin?

. . . According to S. John's explanation, the Living Water that our Lord will give is the Holy Spirit. And it is this Spirit who comes to us who are united to our Lord's divine humanity and who creates in us the desire of spiritual things. He inspires us with spiritual ideals which can only be satisfied by the possession of God.

. . . The Christian life is a revealed life. And it is God that worketh in us both to will and to do his good pleasure. Our life is a life of cooperation with God: he gives the power and we cooperate by the surrender of our wills to him, becoming thus the instruments of his working.

We are mastered by the beauty of the ideal life as our Lord shows it to us and exemplifies it in his own life and in the lives of his saints. The more we yield ourselves and live into the ideal, the more comprehensible it becomes.

BARRY, *INVITATIONS*, 223–24, 226, 231.

HOME-GROWN STUFF

God hates nothing that He has made. He made it because He liked it. His creation is an act of love. And He has made me perhaps to be a temperate plant and to grow in a temperate climate. So what is required of me is to correspond with that climate and environment and to grow the fruit of His Spirit here in the ordinary English garden in which I find myself. . . . We are all rather inclined to be a bit romantic about religion. But God is a realist. He likes home-grown stuff. He asks me for a really good apple, not for a dubious South African peach. So, not lofty thoughts of God, remarkable powers of prayer or displays of devotional fervour or difficult virtues, but gentleness, long-suffering, faithfulness, meekness, a good quality life, will prove I am growing the right way and producing as well as I can the homely fruits for which He asks.

UNDERHILL, *THE FRUITS OF THE SPIRIT*, 39.

JOY AND PEACE

Many of us are accustomed to say each day "I confess to God Almighty, Father, Son and Holy Spirit that I have sinned. . . ." Now what are the respective ways in which we specially sin against the Holy Spirit? All acts, thoughts, tendencies which oppose the pressure of the spiritual life within us and hinder us from bringing forth the Spirit's fruits. So this will include all that diminishes or opposes joy and peace which ought to spread from Christian souls; all deliberate restlessness, fuss, anxiety, all suspiciousness and bitterness, all excursions into the garden to eat religious or political worms, the delightful luxury of spiritual grousing, those meditations on our own unworthiness and unfortunate tempera-ments and so on which we sometimes mistake for humility. All these are sins against the Spirit of Joy and Peace. If we want to be sturdy Christians, strong in spirit, useful to God, all these have got to go.

Again, consider how we allow our small self-interested worries, our self-consciousness, to break our peace—little emotional conflicts, rampant possessiveness and vanity, social or physical disabilities, disap-pointed egotism, sense of being slighted, or anxiety about the future. What about the future? Eternity has no future. It is the Peace of God which no man, however powerful, can take away from him that has it; and he that is born of the Spirit has it now.

UNDERHILL, *THE FRUITS OF THE SPIRIT*, 16–17.

CHRIST THE TEACHER

The development of the apostolic character had about it two character-istics, and I think they are true of all education. Education is brought about in this kind of way. First of all, you watch someone doing the thing you want to do who can do it very well; then you try to do it yourself; and then you bring your attempt to the master for criticism and go away and try again. The apostolic character was formed in that way. The apostles saw Jesus doing things. They saw Him at prayer, for instance, and said, "Lord, teach us to pray." Then we know how they brought to Him their failures in prayer [Matt 17:19–21]. Our spiritual life is to be made up of those two things which we may call meditation and prayer. In our meditation we watch the way our Lord behaves: in our prayer we bring to Him ourselves and the circumstances in which we have to behave.

FATHER ANDREW, *LOVE'S FULFILLMENT*, 89.

DEALING WITH TEMPTATION

Do not fight temptation: ignore it. Except to your confessor or some trusty spiritual friend (and then never for sympathy but only for strength), never speak about your temptations to anyone, and do not speak about them to yourself. Dwelling on them and talking to yourself or other people about them is the worst thing you can do. The positive affirmation of the opposite virtue and the ignoring of the temptation will be your best weapons. Try in a time of temptation to enter into the secret place of the Most High. "He that dwelleth in the secret place of the Most High shall abide under the shadow of the Almighty" [Ps 90:1]. In that secret place you may attain to a union with God which will make the occasion of temptation an occasion of complete spiritual victory.

FATHER ANDREW, *LOVE'S FULFILLMENT*, 137–38.

GROWTH IN HOLINESS

If . . . growth in holiness is to go on unimpeded, it will involve us in two things which, though apparently contradictory, are in fact complementary.

(1) It will involve us in lonely encounter with God. There is a loneli-ness about Christian experience. Just as I am born alone (though into a family), I am born again alone. I die alone. I face God alone. In a sense, I grow alone; for there are spiritual battles which, for all the goodwill in

the world, no one else can fight for me, battles which have to do with pride, and purity, and service and holiness. What it will mean for me when the Wind and the Fire of the Holy Spirit come upon my sinfulness and selfishness, only I can find out in personal encounter with the living God.

(2) It will involve us in close contact with the community of the Holy Spirit, the Church. The Spirit is the Spirit of the Body. It is in the companionship of the Body that each limb grows to its fullness. It is "with all the saints" that we come to know the unknowable love of Christ, not sitting by ourselves in the pious detachment of an "I am better than thou" superiority.

Coggan, Convictions, 186.

THE SANCTIFIED HEART

All the acts of the life of Christ are words by which He invites us to the excellent things of God, for in all He left us an example that we should follow His steps. The mysteries of the being of Christ will unfold themselves to us if we follow the outward actions of the life of Christ. The precepts of Christ seem not plain to the natural heart. We can only see their fitness by the gift of spiritual understanding. It is no wonder if the world rejects the life of Christ, for it rejects the understanding of Christ. It is foolishness unto the world, because it is spiritually discerned. But the life of Christ is straightforward to all who will try and follow it in the strength of His invitation, realizing that the voice which calls them comes from the throne of God. It needs not worldly wisdom. It is the truth of God, which seeks to reproduce itself in the truth of the sanctified heart of the faithful. The way to the glory of the City of God is "a highway, the way of holiness: the unclean shall not pass over it; but it shall be for those: the wayfaring men, though fools, shall not err therein, but the redeemed shall walk there" [Is 35:8].

Benson, Wisdom, 259–60.

CONSECRATE YOUR CHOICES

This is the first and most fundamental of the gifts of the spiritual life: the ability to "take time seriously," to consecrate time, to consecrate our little choices, to look at each day and each act in the light of eternity. That gift of God is what redeems us and our life. And in a world and in a time which feels itself to be so unredeemed and so unredeemable, what greater gift have we, in turn, to give the nations of the world except the gift of freedom and of consecrated choices by which we accept and live up to God's vocation of us?

Our choices are often particularly hard these days; and our minutes are filled with anxieties and distractions almost beyond number. God's gift to us is the ability to take our choices as they come, and to reflect on the great vocation that runs through them all, and then make them with a peaceful heart because we never lose sight of Him who is our goal. Look for Him every day, and make your choices with Him, so that His freedom, which He means to give you, may be yours.

BAYNE, NOW IS THE ACCEPTED TIME, 9.

GOD SPEAKS TO THE SOUL

The spiritual life of a man is a strange thing. That life which is between each man's soul and God has a mysterious history. If it be true that man is made in the image of God, though that image be marred, if it be true that "the light of God lighteth every man that cometh into the world" [John 1:9], if it be true that God wills that all men should be saved, we must know that God speaks to the soul of every man; that He has a message for each man's need, a Gospel of glad tidings for every creature under heaven, that there is no one whom God at some time or other has not mercifully tried to bring unto Himself. In some way suited to the capacity of each, God has spoken and called by His Spirit.

DEKOVEN, SERMONS, 5.

SPIRITUAL ACTIVITY

Spirit is always, by the very essence of its being, an activity, a movement, a quickening power. It cannot exist at all without issuing in act, in motion; wherever it is, it is felt abroad as a wind, strong and masterful, under the pressure of which we see the reeds shake, and the trees bend and bow, and the waters curl and roll: it is felt, sudden and alive, like a flame, under the touch of which things stir, and change, and melt, and kindle, and start, and quiver, and shine. Spirit is a power; and in coming to itself, it has discovered the secret of its power: in finding itself, it has gained an increase of force: in freeing itself from the rule and limit of outward things, it has won to itself new activities, new capacities, new domination. It is more alive than before; and it makes manifest its increase of life by the power which goes out from it; the power of the wind, and of the fire.

Spirit never lives shut up within its own secret pleasure-house, nursing its own musings. It is always a force: if it fails to find scope for action, it loses strength, it wanes. Spiritual emotion cannot sustain itself, unless it become more than an emotion; for spirit holds within it the power to will, its life lies in the free exercise of will; and a will must act, or die. And spirit, too, is love; and love must ever be seeking occasion to show itself, to pour out its gifts, to put itself to use, to carry help: kept to itself, then, unused and ineffective, the love, that is the heart of spirit, withers, and faints.

A revival of spiritual emotion, then, must of necessity involve a revival of spiritual activity. The spirit that is sought and won in the hidden chamber must make itself manifest on the housetops. The spiritual secret that is whispered in darkness must inevitably utter its cry in the broad daylight, must make itself heard in the crowded streets.

This is the law of its life; to win its power from the Father Which seeth in secret, but to exhibit that power in victorious sovereignty over this earth, that our eyes see, and our hands handle.

HOLLAND, *HELPS*, 171–73.

A FORM OF ENERGY

Faith, which is the name by which we call life at its highest, is, as life is, a form of energy. It is life force, seeking to expand into fuller life, seeking to preserve, and realize itself. It is life in open rebellion against death. To say that we live by faith and not by sight, is but another way of saying that we are incomplete, unfinished, not made but in the making, and that we must either grow or die. Faith is the highest form of the will to live. It is not static but dynamic. It must for ever operate against the gravity of doubt; like life, it must always be overcoming obstacles.

STUDDERT KENNEDY, *THE WICKET GATE*, 59.

IN THE STILLNESS

We must seek to build within ourselves a place of silence, into which we can at will retreat; and there seek God, and lay at His Feet the temptation that has to be met with, and the problem that has to be solved. The possession of this place of silence is one of the secrets of personality; and it is in personality above all other things that our present world is poor. Men go about the world, and the thunder and the roar of it get into the very secret places of their souls; and they live for ever in the midst of a blatant and vulgar noise, which poisons the spirit, perverts the judgment and destroys the balance of the intellect, sapping away the foundations of personal freedom, and of fine character. Such a result we have to avoid at all costs. That is the whole object and aim of going to Church. You go to Church, in order that you may take the Church away with you. . . . There is nothing that is more necessary for our souls' salvation than that we should learn, in Church and out of Church, to be still and know that He is God. It is only in the stillness that that great knowledge comes.

STUDDERT KENNEDY, *THE WICKET GATE*, 220–21.

THE ETERNAL GOD

The heart of religion is communion with the eternal. We rise above the tumult and conflict, above even the moral effort, of our normal life to the realm of eternal truth where the ideal is always realised, and perfection alone is actual. Our Lord taught us to pray that God's will may be done on earth as it is in heaven. In our best worship we ascend in heart and mind to the heaven where that Will is always done. We cannot permanently live there. Duty calls us back to the world of moral striving; our faults of character stand out in the clear light of the Divine Presence, and we sink from adoration to penitence even as Isaiah exclaimed, "Woe is me, for I am a man of unclean lips" [Is 6:5], so soon as his eyes had seen the Lord of Hosts and his ears heard the song of the attendant seraphim. But though we cannot dwell permanently on the heights of adoration, all our spiritual health depends upon our rising to them from time to time, and it is good for us to fix in our minds by deliberate meditation the various aspects of our vision in those sacred moments.

Among these, and perhaps chief among them, is the eternity, the changeless perfection, of God. The world in which we live is always changing; it derives its whole meaning from the changes that take place in it. . . .

When we lift our souls to God in adoration we do not have to ascertain afresh each time what degree of perfection He has now attained. He is always the same; our understanding of His glory may develop, but He

Himself is unchanging. . . . Men change; if they cease to change they are dead. But God does not change; His very Life is eternal changelessness.

. . . How shall we rightly approach the eternal God so as to find the repose and strength that are in His eternity? Chiefly by dwelling in thought upon His unvarying holiness. To those who do not also know His love, this is crushing as well as uplifting. But we know that the holy God has sought us in our sin and suffered all our sin could do to draw us out of that sin to Himself. To us, therefore, the holiness of God is uplifting only. . . . Our tendency is always to bombard Him with petitions. We scarcely speak to Him in language of our own except to ask for something. We will not let our very worship lift us above the chances and changes of this fleeting world to the realm of eternal holiness. We think of our desires, our needs, our anxieties, or of the evils that beset the world and the problems that perplex our minds. That is right in its place. But let us take care to give much of our time in prayer to fixing our thoughts on God as He is in Himself.

TEMPLE, *FELLOWSHIP WITH GOD*, 57–59, 67–68.

CREATION, BEAUTY, AND THE ARTS

What is spirituality? Broadly speaking, it is the perception of the spiritual values which bear upon our life, and the development of one's character and personality in ways which reflect and respond to those values. More specifically, a Christian spirituality is the perception of God and an awareness of his presence in all aspects of life, and the conforming of our hearts and minds to Jesus Christ by the power of the Holy Spirit. As it is the created world which surrounds us, and it is through our created senses and faculties that we have knowledge of God, so the ability to perceive spiritual realities in and through their physical manifestations is a basic competence needed by the Christian pilgrim. The knowledge that the Triune God really is in control, this knowledge makes it possible to open our lives to his control and to be nurtured, molded, and brought to maturity in him.

This does not mean a blind, mechanistic obedience or a rigid and impersonal conformity to long sets of rules. Such a view of spirituality would have the effect of dehumanizing us, making us more like animals or machines. On the contrary, the story of creation teaches us to be human, to be men and women who reflect our Maker as we live as persons in community, in harmony with one another and with the world. Indeed we are that unique part of the world which is conscious, which knows God and ourselves and other things.

Catholic Christianity has always recognized and given thanks for the goodness of God as disclosed in creation. We likewise give thanks for our human capacity to perceive at least part of this goodness, to think about it and reflect upon it, and to articulate and share it through words and other forms of expression. Our Catholic Christian heritage affirms and values the fine arts, because this articulation and sharing of beauty is what the painter, poet, musician, architect, or any other kind of artist is trying to do. Art is precisely the way that we lift up the value of things and make it recognizable and communicable. Approached from this direction, we could say that *Christian spirituality is the art of being Christianly human.*

PORTER, *A SONG OF CREATION*, 129–30.

3

Discipleship and Vocation

JOY

Joy is peace for having done that which we ought to have done. . . . To have something to doe, to doe it, and then to Rejoyce in having done it, to embrace a calling, to performe the Duties of that calling, to joy and rest in the peacefull testimony of having done so; this is Christianly done, Christ did it; Angelically done, Angels doe it; Godly done, God does it.

DONNE, *DONNE'S SERMONS*, 85.

CONQUEST OF SELF

There is a beautiful little prayer: "Lord, make us masters of ourselves, in order that we may be servants of others." We can always remember that there is a labour close at hand, and that the most important of all [is] the double task of self-effacement and self-donation. There is no greater labour really than the attainment to a complete self-mastery. All the work of the ministry in our Lord's life, and all the splendour of His courage and patience in the last week of His passion, were without a doubt the fruit of that conquest of self which He had learnt during the years at Nazareth and the days in the wilderness.

FATHER ANDREW, *LOVE'S FULFILLMENT*, 45.

LOVE'S PERFECT SACRIFICE

A questioner asked a native if he would give the Lord a hundred sheep. "Oh, yes," replied the man gaily and glibly, "Gladly would I give the Lord a hundred sheep." "Would you give Him a hundred cows?" repeated the questioner. Again the answer came, "Gladly would I give the Lord a hundred cows." "Would you give Him two pigs?" said the questioner. The man turned on him fiercely. "You know I have two pigs," he said. It is easy to sing hymns and say prayers written by other people, expressive of great sacrifice, when all the while, as the great preacher [Charles H.] Spurgeon once said to his congregation, a man may have his hand in his pocket scratching the side of a coin lest by mistake he should give a florin instead of a penny. It is easy to tell these stories against poor human nature, but it is a comfort at the same time to remember that there is in all of us the divine spark which can appreciate love's perfect sacrifice and can learn in the school of Christ the lesson of dying to self-love and living to God.

FATHER ANDREW, LOVE'S FULFILLMENT, 180–81.

OUR EXAMPLE

Let every one be watchful over his life, that his conversation be according to his profession. If we walk disorderly, we shall not walk alone: our example will draw others after it; and their sins we shall answer for. Lucifer fell not alone: he drew company from heaven with him. Jeroboam, being sinful, made Israel to sin. And he is burned in the hand with that mark of horror, for a warning to all succeeding ages: "Jeroboam the son of Nebat, that made Israel to sin" [2 Kgs 13]. Let us beware that we play not Simeon and Levi, and so make our father Jacob to be loathed of the Canaanites. We profess Christ and true Christianity: let us not through our lewd life be a slander to our Saviour, and a shame to his gospel. Watch therefore.

SANDYS, SERMONS, 397.

MIRACLES

Miracle occurs to a world prepared for miracle; open to miracle; a world that, by its movements, invites miraculous entrance. Does it not occur to us? Does no miracle reach us? Then this forces on us a practical question—Are you and I prepared? Are our souls open to it? Is our inner life such as to evoke some special act from God? Have we made motions, starts, struggles, to which it will be no surprise if God responds by efforts, starts, motions, of His own? It is we who must be in movement if a movement of God is to advance to meet us. It is our belief that must be stirring, if Christ is to do any mighty work in our midst. Motion will answer to motion—God's motion without to our motion within. If we do but step out, if we will but make the venture, then the new strange world opens, the new strange miraculous life begins. Where we end, God begins. Just where our effort dies away in feebleness, God lays hold of it, and saves it. Just where we stumble, and reel, God's Hand is reached out to catch us. Just where we grow dizzy, Christ's Voice reassures: "I am here; be not afraid." Just where we swoon into pain and death, He is there by our side, "Who died, and was buried; and behold, He is alive for evermore." This is the everlasting life of inward miracle, which each one of us may know, and taste, and learn, and feel, that so we may accept, with ease and joy, that record of outward miracle asserted in the Gospels, which is thus confirmed by our own experiences.

HOLLAND, HELPS, 6–7.

GIVING ONESELF

It is perfectly possible for us to behave kindly, justly, and correctly toward one another yet withhold that giving of the "self" which is the essence of love. Married people will perhaps more easily appreciate what I am trying to say. A husband may behave with perfect kindness and consideration toward his wife; . . . he may do more than his share of the household chores, and indeed he may do all the things which an ideal husband is supposed to do. But if he withholds "himself" the marriage will be impoverished. Women who seem to know these things intuitively would infinitely prefer the husband to be less kind, considerate, and self-sacrificing if they were only sure that he with all his imperfections and maddening ways gave "himself" in love in the marriage. This principle applies to some extent to all human relationships, and I am quite certain that it is this costly, self-giving love which Paul had in mind in 1 Corinthians 13. Many, even among Christians, shrink from it, not I think because they are afraid to give but because they are afraid that their gift will not be appreciated; in short, that they may be hurt. But surely this is the risk that love must always take, and without this giving of the self with all the risks that that entails, love is a poor pale imitation. "Consider him" [Heb 12:3], writes the author of the Epistle to the Hebrews, and if we do we find this is precisely the sort of rejectable, vulnerable love Christ lived and died to prove.

PHILLIPS, THE NEWBORN CHRISTIAN, 121–22.

A TRANSFORMING FRIENDSHIP

The Church has a great commission and command from its Lord. When we examine that command, to go to the ends of the earth and proclaim the Gospel to every creature, it poses a terrifying question which was asked first by a Roman official. In the dock before him stood a despised and brutally beaten prisoner. An angry mob was shouting for his blood, and none there was to champion His cause or testify in His behalf. Armed with the might of Rome, Pilate is uneasy. He senses there is more in this situation than meets the eye, and he asks a question: "What shall I then do with Jesus, which is called the Christ?" Appalling answers have been given in the centuries since that question. Some have sought to ignore Him as though He had never been and is not now. He will not be ignored. Others have admired Him, found great solace in His teaching, and sought to keep Him for themselves. But this attempt has never succeeded. When men seek to keep Him for themselves, He does again what He did in the ancient town where He was brought up—passes through their midst and goes on His way. Selfishness is the most self-destroying of all the powers known to man. Men and nations, groups and classes, have sought to keep Him for themselves. How baffling it is to discover that all these are gone. He remains.

Others, yet again, have sought to share Him, His love and His power and His life. In so doing they have discovered that they have entered into a transforming friendship. There is no other in all history like it. Life knows no equal prize. Think what it did for that little company of disciples. Once they were convinced—and they were not easily convinced—that He is the Truth for life, they become other men. That fear which sent them into hiding was transformed into courage which made them the men of their day. Their uncertainty and doubt were, by the alchemy of His love, changed into radiant assurance and blazing faith. Lips which were silent in the hiding place now proclaim in the market place that Christ is Lord. Lives before soiled by sin, are cleansed and purified.

What did this? A triumphant friendship which so changed men that men could find but one sensible explanation—they had been with Jesus. This friendship changed a renegade tax collector into a chronicler of eternal truth; changed a narrow nationalist into a preacher of the universal love of God; changed an accessory to murder into a bearer of life; changed a rich and luxurious and spoiled young son into the little brother of the poor.

This, my Brethren, is what the world needs today—this transforming friendship. This we are sent by God to make possible for all the sons of men.

Powell, "The Bishop's Address" (1960), 98–99.

NOT ALONE

"But what can I do?" The answer is, "Nothing worthwhile," if we think of the task as being our task alone. It is not ours alone. "Lo," said Jesus, "I am with you always, even unto the end of the world." In ancient days a humble, Asian Monk observed the world about him. One day he wandered into the vastness of the Roman Colosseum, then crowded with people come to see a gladiatorial combat. What he saw filled his heart with horror, and with awe. With the crowd, he left behind this place of butchery, but he did not leave behind the effect which that butchery had on him. This, and the deep thought which he took back to his cell, gave him no rest by night or by day. What could he do against the customs of the mightiest of the empires? Nothing, if alone. He went back to that horrid spectacle. This time, not alone. He went in the conscious companionship of the Son of God. The roar of the crowd swelled its passion for blood—the gates were opened. The gladiatorial horror began again. Rising from his place, he sprang into the arena and sought to separate the contestants. The howling mob rose to its feet and stoned him to death. But is he gone? No. Telemachus, his deed, his death, mark the evening of the gladiatorial shows. What can one person do? No one knows until in conscious companionship with God's Son he dares everything for that righteousness which is in Jesus Christ our Lord, who braved the cross that we might live.

Powell, "The Bishop's Address" (1961), 101–2.

A SIN-BEARING PEOPLE

If the Church is a Church indeed, it is a body of sin-bearing people; people who love with the love of God that is shed abroad in their hearts, and who, because they love, are compelled to bear the burden of the world's sins. They are a body of people who can forgive because they are forgiven, who have been loved into being lovers. Unless the Church of Christ is by love so united with the whole of mankind, that the sin of the world is the sin of the Church, the disgrace of the world, the disgrace of the Church, the shame of the world, the shame of the Church—then it is not a Church at all. However highly organized, however doctrinally orthodox, however correct ecclesiastically, it is not a Church, but a counterfeit, if it does not bear the sin of the world.

STUDDERT KENNEDY, *THE WICKET GATE*, 199.

THERE IS ONLY ONE MINISTRY

The most urgent truth about the Church is what is hidden in our fumbling phrase, "the ministry of the laity." It is not a phrase I like very much, for it suggests that there are many ministries, and this is really not true. There is only one ministry—Christ's ministry. He is the only Minister there is in the Church. It is He Who receives the baby into His great Body in baptism; it is He Who puts His hands over mine in confirmation or ordination; it is He Who stands at the altar and breaks the Bread. He is the Bishop and Shepherd of our souls; He is the great High Priest Who has passed into the heavens; He is the Lamb Who offered His life, wholly and completely, and showed us what it is to be free. There is no way of chopping up His ministry and giving bits of it to one or to another.

Because Christ is One and there is only one ministry, then priest and layman alike need to learn that their separate lives are only two sides of the same coin—that the great imperatives of the Gospel lie over both—that both together must fulfill the work of Christ in this world.

BAYNE, *NOW IS THE ACCEPTED TIME*, 79.

BE NOT ASHAMED

Never be ashamed of thy birth, or thy parents, or thy trade, or thy present employment, for the meanness or poverty of any of them; and when there is an occasion to speak of them, such an occasion as would invite you to speak of any thing that pleases you, omit it not; but speak as readily and indifferently of thy meanness, as of thy greatness. Primislaus, the first king of Bohemia, kept his country shoes always by him, to remember from whence he was raised: and Agathocles, by the furniture of his table, confessed that from a potter he was raised to be the king of Sicily.

TAYLOR, *HOLY LIVING*, 75.

THE QUEST OF THE SELF

It is easy to say, "Be yourself," if you could find the self you are supposed to be: but what is it? Some people think that they are being themselves, and wonderfully sincere, if they identify themselves with their worst and most primitive passions. But that is to be little better than an animal, and how can I be myself by being a beast? I am a man, surely, and how can I be myself by forgetting my noblest part? Where is the sincerity in a man's being a beast? Yet if I attempt to follow a higher ideal of myself, how easily do I become a prig or a hypocrite.

The saint has solved the problem of sincerity in the sole possible way by turning to God, the great I AM, and accepting the self his creator designed for him. And the quest of the self God has meant each of us to be is like the quest of happiness (which is indeed much the same thing)—it is not found by looking for it. We do not ask of God, "What sort of person did you mean me to be?"—we say to him "Lord, what wilt thou have me to do?"

FARRER, *A Celebration of Faith*, 199–200.

VOCATION

The one question is, whether God calls us: it is not whether we feel fit or no. If God gives us the call, God will give us the grace. We may underestimate ourselves, as well as over-estimate ourselves. St. Paul said, "Who is sufficient for these things?" If St. Paul, how much more we? The question is not as to anything in the past or present; but as to the call of God. If God calls us, He will fit us. When God put our soul into the bodies which we received of our parents, He had His own special purpose for each of us. He willed each of us to be saved in doing our own appointed work. He had us and our whole selves to be formed in our own special way. We sometimes hear of a person mistaking his profession; of his being, e.g., a good lawyer spoiled, a good man of business spoiled, i.e. he had missed the employment of life for which God adapted [him].

I cannot tell what your calling is: I know only certain outward dispositions: hold up your soul as a sheet of white paper to God, for Him to write on it what He wills. He has promised to hear prayer: say with St. Augustine, "Give what Thou commandest, and command what Thou willest." Do not hurry, but pray Him to teach you.

PUSEY, *Spiritual Letters*, 23.

FELLOW WORKERS WITH GOD

Spirits of cowardice and self-indulgence will be about us every day, whispering to us the manifold arguments which there are against hope. "Why should you work? What good is to come of it all? Why should you believe? What have you to believe in? Why should you look to be happy? Does it not seem as if all these multitudes were born to be miserable?" The last is the point at which we should begin our answer to these suggestions. You ask me what title I can make out to happiness? None. You ask me how I can prove myself better than the suffering multitude? I can offer no such proofs. You ask me then what I have to believe in? I answer, In Him who created all these myriads and me, in Him who works even in me by His Spirit to care for these as well as for myself. I believe in Him who brings the light out of darkness every morning, who causes His sun to shine on the just and on the unjust, on the good and on the evil. You ask me what is the good of work? I answer, If this is my belief, I am bound also to believe that every work from the beginning of the universe until now has been in some way or other for the manifestation of the glory of Him who created it. I am bound to believe that no work of the hands, no work of the brain, has been useless. Every student of nature, of history, of language, of the world without or of the world within, so far as he is faithful, so far as he suffers no prejudices of other men, no prejudices of his own, to interfere with his search for truth in his own direction, must be a minister of God, one who is contributing in some way to the manifestation of His glory. Every man who is toiling honestly in the field or at the loom must be contributing to the manifestation of His glory. If any are unfaithful or dishonest, He will accomplish His purpose, but it is our privilege, if we will, to enter into His purpose, to be fellow-workers with him. And every one who claims that privilege must cherish hope, must treat as devils and powers of darkness all that would tempt him to despair.

MAURICE, *LESSONS OF HOPE*, 151–53.

LOVE SERVES

When a man loves he serves. Be the terms of the service never so exacting, be the conditions of the service never so imperative, still if a man loves he serves. . . . And . . . service is certainly the characteristic of our Lord's love among men. He says emphatically, "I am among you as one that serveth" [Luke 22:27]. He took upon Himself the form of a servant and became obedient unto death. . . . Now, the reason why when a man loves he serves, and the reason why because our Lord loved us, He came as a servant, is this, that love is the gift of self to the object of its love. Love is unlike passion in this respect. It is something more than passion. Passion desires to have the object of its consideration fastened upon itself. Not so love. Love is the gift of self. In this it is distinct from passion. . . . When a man loves he gives . . . himself.

STANTON, FAITHFUL STEWARDSHIP, 152–53.

WORK

Don't be too easily convinced that God really wants you to do all sorts of work you needn't do. Each must do his duty "in that state of life to which God has called him" [1 Cor 7:17, 20].

. . . [T]here can be intemperance in work just as in drink. What feels like zeal may be only fidgets or even the flattering of one's self-importance. As MacDonald says "In holy things may be unholy greed." And by doing what "one's station and its duties" does not demand, one can make oneself less fit for the duties it does demand and so commit some injustice. Just you give Mary a little chance as well as Martha!

LEWIS, LETTERS TO AN AMERICAN LADY, 50–51.

4

Prayer

SEASONS FOR PRAYER

. . . God hath made no decree to distinguish the seasons of his mercies; In paradise, the fruits were ripe, the first minute, and in heaven it is alwaies Autumne, his mercies are ever in their maturity. We ask *panem quotidianum,* our daily bread, and God never sayes you should have come yesterday, he never sayes, you must againe to morrow, but *to day if you will heare his voice,* to day he will heare you. If some King of the earth have so large an extent of Dominion, in North and South, as that he hath Winter and Summer together in his Dominions, so large an extent East and West, as that he hath day and night together in his Dominions, much more hath God mercy and judgement together: He brought light out of darknesse, not out of a lesser light; he can bring thy Summer out of Winter, though thou have no Spring; though in the wayes of fortune, or understanding, or conscience, thou have been benighted till now, wintred and frozen, clouded and eclypsed, damped and benummed, smothered and stupified till now, now God comes to thee, not as in the dawning of the day, not as in the bud of the spring, but as the Sun at noon to illustrate all shadowes, as the sheaves in harvest, to fill all penuries, all occasions invite his mercies, and all times are his seasons.

DONNE, *DONNE'S SERMONS,* 139–40.

HOW SHALL I LIVE?

We must pray, for prayer is neither more nor less than living with God. Shall I live today of myself and by myself or shall I live it with God? Doubtless, whether or not I live it with God, God lives it with me—but that only makes it the more monstrous that I should not live it with him.

Prayer is just living with God: looking at him, regarding his will, reaching out our hands for the blessings he is so eager to give, bringing our action into his. We must pray. If you cannot pray, come and ask for help. What could be more natural, than for a Christian to say to a priest, may I make a date to talk to you about my prayers? What else are we for?

FARRER, THE END OF MAN, 106.

PRAYING AND LOVING

For there is nothing that makes us love a man so much as praying for him; and when you can once do this sincerely for any man, you have fitted your soul for the performance of everything that is kind and civil toward him. This will fill your heart with a generosity and tenderness that will give you a better and sweeter behavior than anything that is called fine breeding and good manners.

By considering yourself as an advocate with God for your neighbors and acquaintances, you would never find it hard to be at peace with them yourself. It would be easy to you to bear with and forgive those for whom you particularly implored the divine mercy and forgiveness.

LAW, A SERIOUS CALL, 292.

WHEN WE SAY THE LORD'S PRAYER

Notice that we are taught to pray not: "Give me my daily bread," but "Give us our daily bread." We pray to the Father of all for the whole human family. That is why, if we are going to be literal-minded, it makes good sense for us, last thing at night, to pray "Give us this day our daily bread." For when we are going to bed, the sun is rising and a new day is beginning in other countries and in other parts of the world. When we say the Lord's Prayer, we are praying for them as well as for ourselves.

Of course, we could not pray with integrity that all our fellow human beings may have their daily bread, if we were not prepared to do everything in our power to see that they do have it. . . .

VIDLER, WINDSOR SERMONS, 116.

CONFESSING THE TRUTH ABOUT OURSELVES

When Thomas said to his fellow-disciples, "unless I see and touch, I shall not believe," what do you think it was? Was it a refusal, or a boast, or a confession? A refusal—I won't believe: or a boast—I'm too clever to believe: or a confession—I shan't be able to believe? He was a friend and disciple of Christ's, who had risked his life with him: how could he refuse to believe that God had raised him from the dead? or how boast of sceptical detachment, who had committed himself to a cause, body and soul? No, surely it was more like a confession: That's the sort of man I *am*; I shan't be able to believe, unless I believe my own hands, and eyes. If, when he said this, Thomas was telling the truth, he could hardly have done better: do you think he would have done better if he had lied? If he had pretended to believe, when he didn't? When we come to Christ in our prayer, shall we tell him a pack of lies? Shall we pretend all sorts of noble sentiments we do not have: pretend to believe in him as firmly as we believe our own existence, pretend to care for his holy will as warmly and constantly as we care for our own comforts and ambitions? Of course not; for whom could we hope to deceive? Not him: we could only deceive ourselves. No, we will confess ourselves as we are, and know that he will treat us on our level, and according to our need, as he did Thomas: reach hither thy finger, and feel my hands; reach hither thy hand, and put it in my side: go not in lack of faith but believe.

FARRER, *A CELEBRATION OF FAITH*, 79.

PREPARATION FOR PRAYER

So we turn to prayer quietly, confidently, as God's beloved. . . .

Our prayer will be transformed if we always take time for a moment or two of preparation—if we reflect on the greatness and the mercy and the nearness of the God to whom we are coming. Instead of plunging immediately into distracted petitions about our own affairs . . . we shall begin by waiting upon God in quiet faith. Our prayer will be more real, and far more effective, if we remember to make a brief pause for preparation, if for a few moments we stop talking, and try to hold ourselves still before God. . . . [We should] put ourselves and our needs into God's hands, and . . . . seek first of all that he may be glorified. Once we have entered into this rest . . . our hearts will be strangely lightened, we shall find that we are less self-centred, less troubled by the sight of our sins and miseries, for we are now more willing to face the truth about ourselves.

WYON, *PRAYER*, 43.

LIFE AND PRAYER

Our life is our prayer. Our prayer is our effort to bring all things in our life under the direction and rule of the Holy Spirit, but our life is really our prayer. We can only give back to God the kind of day His providence first gives to us, but the giving to Him of that kind of day is our prayer. If God gives you a day of toil, you can only give Him a day of toil, and that day of toil is your prayer. Your prayer is the love you put into it. If God gives you a day of conflict, you can only give Him a day of conflict, and that day of conflict is your prayer, and what you call your prayer is again the love you put into it to bring it under the direction and rule of the Holy Spirit. If God gives you a day of joy, then you can give Him your gratitude in the enjoyment of it, and that is your prayer.

FATHER ANDREW, *LOVE'S FULFILLMENT*, 93.

PRAYER AND BREVITY

It is a common saying; If a man does not know how to pray, let him go to sea, and that will teach him. And we have a notable instance of what kind of prayers men are taught in that school, even in the disciples themselves, when a storm arose, and the sea raged, and the ship was ready to be cast away, in the 8th of Matthew. In which case, we do not find that they fell presently to harangue it about seas and winds, and that dismal face of things that must needs appear all over the devouring element at such a time: All which, and the like, might, no doubt, have been very plentiful topics of eloquence to a man, who should have looked upon these things from the shore; or discoursed of wrecks and tempests safe and warm in his parlour. But these poor wretches, who were now entering (as they thought) into the very jaws of death, struggling with the last efforts of nature, upon the sense of a departing life; and consequently, could neither speak nor think any thing low or ordinary in such a condition, presently rallied up, and discharged the whole concern of their desponding souls in that short prayer, of but three words, though much fuller, and more forcible, than one of three thousand, in the 25th verse of the forementioned chapter; Save us Lord, or we perish. Death makes short work when it comes, and will teach him, who would prevent it, to make shorter. For surely no man, who thinks himself aperishing, can be at leisure to be eloquent; or judge it either sense or devotion, to begin a long prayer, when, in all likelihood, he shall conclude his life before it.

SOUTH, *SERMONS*, 452–53.

FIRST THOUGHTS

We wake morning by morning to a new life. The cares and thoughts of yesterday have been buried in our sleep; the world around us is still hushed; the turmoil of life has not yet come back to haunt us. We should deal reverently, then, with our first thoughts, beware how we awaken in ourselves any of the trains of plans, or business, or occupations, which take up our day. They are yet at a distance from us, and we have more power over them. Stop their first inroad, turn from them reverently to God before one thought have awakened its fellow; that so thou mayst secure undisturbed thy first prayers, wherein thou committest thy whole self, soul, body, and spirit, for the day to God. Our minds are holy things; they are the temples of God, and so, for His honour's sake who has so hallowed them, we should be on our guard what we allow to enter there.

PUSEY, *SELECTIONS*, 11–12.

MEDITATE DAILY

Meditate daily on the things of eternity, and by the grace of God do something daily which thou wouldst wish to have done when the Day of Judgment comes. Eternity fades quickly from sight, amid the mists and clouds of this world. Heaven is above our heads, yet we see it not with eyes fixed on the earth.

PUSEY, *SELECTIONS*, 13.

HELP, LORD!

So many say, and feel, it is so difficult to pray. If they mean to make prayers, or to pray prayers, I admit it requires mental exertion, for it is a spiritual exercise.

But when they say "I can't pray," then I join issue with them at once and proclaim the contradiction. I say you can't help praying, you can't help praying any more than you can help breathing. Breathing is the necessity of a living body, and prayer is the necessity of a living soul. When you say, "I felt I couldn't pray to-day," I know you have prayed. Your wish was a prayer, your very need was an appeal that God recognized, although never a word you uttered.

... Help, Lord! It is the natural cry of the created to the Creator, of the finite to the Infinite. It belongs to "the whole creation that groaneth and travaileth in pain together until now" [Rom 8:22]. It is an appeal to the fountain head of all existence, God.

... A man doesn't cry for help unless he wants it. And the cry is put into the heart of God. When temptation comes, the spirit of prayer goes. Oh, cry out "Lord help me!"

STANTON, SERMON OUTLINES, 147, 149.

INTERCESSION

To intercede is to bear others on our heart in God's presence. Intercession becomes not the bombardment of God with requests so much as the bringing of our desires within the stream of God's own compassion. For His compassion flows ceaselessly towards the world, but it seems to wait upon the co-operation of human wills. This occurs partly when God's creatures do the things that God desires to be done, and partly by prayers, which are also channels of God's compassion. In intercession therefore we dwell first upon the loving-kindness of God in recollection, praise and thankfulness. It is there that intercession begins, dwelling upon God's greatness and flowing from the act of worship.

RAMSEY, GLORY DESCENDING, 91.

5

Holy Scripture

AN IMPERFECT CHURCH

If we read them with our eyes open St. Paul's Epistles, and especially that to the Galatians, are very disillusioning documents on the history of the Early Church. In Galatians II, for instance, we see that, in spite of the great torrent of divine Holiness poured out at Pentecost, Peter is still shifty and quarrelsome, Paul still contentious and hot-tempered, and so forth. Yet it was out of the society which is described there that the Gospels came with their exquisite beauty and demand for limitless love, and their stern reality. It was a society full of petty disputes and always worrying about Church finance, in fact very like the Church to-day. At any rate this bit of history can teach us long-suffering in respect of our imperfect ecclesiastical surroundings—really not any worse than the Asiatic Church of the first century—we are not to give them up as hopeless or discuss them with bitterness. It is not always the purest soil in which saints grow best. If God can and does accept, use and indwell an imperfect Church, then we might accept it too and not be fastidious.

UNDERHILL, *THE FRUITS OF THE SPIRIT*, 23.

THE OLD WAY

People now are trying to make themselves happy without religion, but it is a hollow, heartless kind of happiness, not worthy of the name. I believe the love of God must stand first, and then, in God, we can love one another. People want to have social security and comfort, but without religion, without the Church. We must hold fast to the old way of the love of God, and the love of one another as taught us in the Bible and the Prayer Book, and we want the Church for the sake of the ministry of the Word and Sacraments, by which God teaches us, and gives us His grace.

KING, *SPIRITUAL LETTERS*, 30.

THE FUNCTION OF THE GOSPELS

The Gospels have this one aim, to enable us to know Who it is in Whom we are asked to believe. . . . It is natural . . . for us to wish to have more written. But do we not deceive ourselves if we think that, by having more, we should find our perplexities cleared, our hesitations dismissed? Judas saw and heard far more—saw and heard all these many things which John has left unwritten; and, after all, he went away and communed with the chief priests how he might betray Him for thirty pieces of silver.

No! there is enough in our brief Gospels to challenge us with a living Presence Which we must face; and, having faced, must either follow or flee. And it is not the book, but that living Presence, in which we are to believe, on which we are to rely. That is its moral challenge. There it stands and moves and speaks. We can all feel it, as it draws near, as it passes by. Not by arguments, not by explanations, not by persuasions, not by these weapons, does it make its attack. No! but by being what it is. "I am what I am"; "I am that which I also told you"; "Whom say ye that I . . . am?" That is the Voice that speaks through the written records—speaks as none other ever spoke. It is the voice of a living Man, not of a book—using a book through which to speak, but Himself the Key of the written Word; Himself the Power in the book; Himself the Argument and the Appeal; Himself the Soul of the record. Though all the books that the world could contain were written about Him, the situation would still be the same. At the end, when we had read them all, the one question would remain to be answered. "After all that has been written, wilt thou follow Me; wilt thou trust Me; wilt thou obey Me; wilt thou put thy soul in My hands?"

That question—that challenge—is just what you and I are facing now.

The words that we read in the printed page have passed into the mouth of One Who is pressing for an immediate response: "I am the Vine"; "I am the Good Shepherd"; "Come unto Me"; "My peace I give unto you"; "I am the Resurrection and the Life." Oh! now for the brave act of the soul, now for the movement of the adventurous will, now for the spring of faith! No book will give us that; but only the Spirit of the living God, that works at once through the book, and also within our hearts—the eternal Spirit of the ascended Lord, that takes of His and shows it unto us.

HOLLAND, *HELPS*, 27–29.

THE CHRIST OF ALL

In the gospels we see in Jesus two lives. They are in strong contrast, yet not in disagreement. He dwells in and reveals His father: He also lives a human life. To see that these are one we must have clearly in view why and how He became man. He became man, as the deliberate act of God, for our recovery. God must be revealed: the ideal of human nature must be shown forth. Humanity must therefore reflect the perfect God perfectly. His human nature was allowed to be subject to limitation, without defacing or distorting the revelation made. When He teaches, we may depend upon what He teaches; else the purpose of His coming would be marred. On the other hand, He is to show a true manhood. This must be tried, must progress, must he perfected. Human experience must be possible: hence He is without such divine rights and powers as make that impossible.

Further, we have to understand the method of the incarnation. S. Paul calls it a self-emptying. Christ existed before the incarnation in the "form" of God. This word means the "permanent, essential character." This life was His of right: yet He did not clutch at it as a prize. For love He gave it up. He emptied Himself to take up the human life, the "form" of a servant. The outward fashion, too, of man He took. Thus remaining an unchanged person, He abandoned certain prerogatives of divine existence. Elsewhere S. Paul calls it a self-beggary. On God's part, too, there is a surrender, a giving up of the Son. In accordance with this the record seems to assure us that our Lord in His mortal life was not habitually living in the exercise of omniscience.

Is this intelligible? In a measure it is. We, too, in our sympathy enter into the conditions of another's life. The teacher thus deals with the child; the educated with the savage. We can thus enter somewhat into it, though, of course, we can never understand all. . . .

Jesus Christ, then, is the Son of man, like and yet unlike to ourselves. In what is He unlike? (1) He is sinless. He was assailed, but He rejected temptation, not because He felt no force in it, but because His will followed unhesitatingly the Spirit of God. And since He was sinless,

He was free. Sin is no part of man's true nature, for sin had no place in Christ. Through Him we, too, look forward to a like freedom. (2) In Jesus Christ humanity was perfect. Man was made imperfect, fitted only to develop freely. In Christ man is completely God's image. (3) Jesus Christ is the universal man. He can be claimed by both sexes, all classes, all nations. . . .

In Christ we find our hopes for man justified. There is much in man to dishearten us; there is much in ourselves. . . . [Christ] is our authority, our example, our new life. The hope of progress for each man and all men lies with those who in simple loyalty follow His guidance.

GORE, WHY WE CHRISTIANS BELIEVE, 48–51.

THE EVANGELISTS

St. Luke is noted for his instinct for souls. His Gospel has been named the Gospel of Mercy, because it is so full of incidents of our Lord's love of sinners. His is a Gospel of sunshine; without him we should have known little of the holy Childhood; and to him, the first artist of the Church, we fitly owe the three songs of the Gospel, the *Magnificat*, the *Benedictus*, and the *Nunc Dimittis*. He was the Evangelist of the sacred Infancy, as St. John of the Lord's Divinity, St. Matthew and St. Mark of the active life of our blessed Lord.

PUSEY, SELECTIONS, 20.

THE FELLOWSHIP OF THE CHURCH

The fellowship of the Church can indeed manifest the glory of God to the consciences of men and women; but it does so not by providing something for impenitent human beings to like and admire, but by being a fellowship so filled with God Himself that their conscience is pierced by God's love and judgement. Thus the gospel of the glory of God is always very near to human beings, and yet always very far from them: near, because the divine image is in every human person and the gospel is the true meaning of the human person; far, because it is heard only by faith and repentance, which overthrow all human self-glorying.

RAMSEY, GLORY DESCENDING, 20.

THE CHRISTIAN STRUGGLE

If the Gospel only gave precept and example, it would not be the Gospel. It must reveal a new life, a life of which we may be partakers, as real and true as throbbing pulse and aching brain, and muscle and nerves, and flesh and blood. It must not merely bid us gaze upon a spiritual world, and tell us of its duties and its happiness, but take us into it, and first give to man the germ of the higher life it demands. If it ask for faith, it must give faith; if it ask for sacrifice, it must give the power to offer it; if it ask for victory, it must give the ability to conquer, and must only demand of us that we should use the gifts aright.

In short, the struggle which God has appointed for man requires, and must have, a supernatural life and supernatural gifts. St. Paul says: "I am crucified with Christ. . . . Christ liveth in me. The life which I now life in the flesh, I live by faith in the Son of God" [Gal 2:20]. The Cross of Christ, the life of Christ—not things of the past, but of the present; not His alone, but ours; a death with Him and a life with Him—these alone make struggle possible.

DeKoven, Sermons, 206–7.

THE GOSPEL REMEDY

The Gospel, on the other hand, is like a faithful physician, applying his remedies in due season, whether such remedies please the patient or no; and very careful, if I may so speak, to look after his diet and daily habits continually denying him things which he most covets, and urging on him practices which are most irksome, and most contrary to his turn of mind. It is the patient's nature, the nature of us all, to be taken up with things present, and care little for things invisible; but the physician, the Gospel, keeps calling on us day and night to remember that things invisible are all in all. Our disease is, to think well of ourselves, and to count it hard when we are bid to be in earnest, lowly and meek, and to depend entirely on Christ our Saviour. No wonder that we loathe such a remedy as the Gospel, of which the self-denying doctrines are the very sum and substance. . . . The sweet, and amiable, and useful spirit of the Gospel will always obtain for it a certain degree of favour; but further than this, people will not go; and when the *whole* Gospel, the *whole* counsel and will of God, is pressed upon them earnestly and without reserve, they will presently begin to be vexed and angry, and, as far as God's providence allows, will in some way or another contrive to persecute its teachers. For the *whole* Gospel of Jesus Christ, the *whole* counsel and message of God, is not only a kind and gentle, but it is also a strict self-denying law. It looks to people's good, not to their satisfaction: it cares not whether they are pleased or angry, provided the great end be accomplished, of leading them, practically, and in earnest, to care for their souls, and love God's truth, and amend their ways accordingly. It is as absurd to expect such a message to be generally popular, as if a physician were to expect that his patients should generally like the medicines he gives them.

KEBLE, *SERMONS*, 42–45.

PERVERTED INGENUITY

[T]here is nothing more miserable, as specimens of perverted ingenuity, than the attempts of certain commentators and preachers to find remote and recondite and intended allusions to Christ everywhere [in the Bible]. For example, they chance to find in the construction of the temple the fusion of two metals, and this they conceive is meant to show the union of Divinity with Humanity in Christ. If they read of coverings to the tabernacle, they find implied the doctrine of imputed righteousness. If it chance that one of the curtains of the tabernacle be red, they see in that the prophecy of the blood of Christ. If they are told that the kingdom of heaven is a pearl of great price, they will see it in the allusion that, as a pearl is the production of animal suffering, so the kingdom of heaven is produced by the sufferings of the Redeemer.

ROBERTSON, *LIVING THOUGHTS*, 20–21.

INSPIRATION

The inspiration of the Bible is a large subject. I hold it to be inspired, not dictated. It is the Word of God—the words of man: as the former, perfect; as the latter, imperfect. God the Spirit, as the Sanctifier, does not produce absolute perfection of human character; God the Spirit, as an Inspirer, does not produce absolute perfection of human knowledge; and for the same reason in both cases—the human element which is mixed up. . . . Let us take . . . the history of the creation. Now, I hold that a spiritual revelation from God *must* involve scientific incorrectness: it could not be from God unless it did. Suppose that the cosmogony had been given in terms which would satisfy our present scientific knowledge, or say, rather, the terms of absolute scientific truth: It is plain that, in this case, the men of that day would have rejected its authority; they would have said, "Here is a man who tells us the earth goes round the sun: and the sky, which we see to be . . . fixed and not far up, is infinite space, with no *firmament* at all, and so on. Can we trust one in matters unseen who is manifestly in error in things seen and level to the senses? Can we accept his revelation about God's nature and man's duty when he is wrong in things like these?" Thus, the faith of this and subsequent ages must have been purchased at the expense of the unbelief of all previous ages. I hold it, therefore, as a proof of inspiration of the Bible, and divinely wise, to have given . . . a revelation concerning the truths of the soul and its relation to God in popular and incorrect language. Do not mistake that word incorrect: incorrect is one thing, false another. It is scientifically incorrect to say that the sun rose this morning; but it is not false, because it conveys all that is required, for the nonce, to be known about the fact, time, etc. And if God were giving a revelation in this present day, He would give it in modern phraseology, and the men He inspired would talk of sunrise, sunset, etc. Men of science smile at the futile attempts to reconcile Moses and geology. I give up the attempt at once, and say the inspiration of the Bible remains intact for all that—nay, it would not have been inspired except on this condition of incorrectness.

ROBERTSON, LIVING THOUGHTS, 21–22.

VISIONS AND SYMBOLS

Every Easter as it comes round should imprint upon us the truth that in the end . . . good will prevail.

Every Easter this great truth should become more clear to us through the experience of our lives, and so deepen our insight into the teaching of the Word of God. Such is gloriously the teaching of the last book of the Bible, the Apocalypse, the Revelation of S. John the Divine. In its frequent references and use of symbols it traverses the whole course of Revelation, gathering up, as it were, the whole purport of the real mind and Will of God: it presents to our view the picture of the downfall of Babylon, that great city, the representative of the world; and not only so, but the beast, and the false prophet, and the devil, the great deceiver, all are finally overthrown, and then there stands before us the new Jerusalem, in all the beauty of holiness, the city of God, the city that hath foundations, the eternal city.

This teaches us clearly that the forces, personal and impersonal, which have inspired mankind with false views of life . . . will, in the end, be completely subjugated! It is the victory of right over wrong, of the truth over falsehood, of good over evil: the revelation of the victorious Christ. Such is the irresistible lesson which the last book of our Bible leaves with us.

No doubt much of the teaching of the book of the Revelation is conveyed to us in visions and symbols and signs, many of which we are unable to interpret with certainty. Much of the book is prophetic, and looks forward to days and circumstances of which we as yet have no experience; many minor points, too, as in our Lord's parables, we cannot use for certain as the proof of doctrine, yet, by comparing Scripture with Scripture, we can see the meaning to be generally agreeable to the Word of God.

So these difficulties are no sufficient excuse for putting the book aside as altogether unintelligible. The book, like the rest of Scripture, is written for our learning, and is given by the inspiration of God, and is profitable for doctrine, for reproof, for correction in righteousness.

KING, *EASTER SERMONS*, 96–97.

6

The Sacramental Life

THE POWER OF SYMBOL

Many have owed their conversion to the eye and the ear, engaged by some symbolical presentment of vital truth, who would have been deaf to the most forcible appeal to the logical faculty; and this because they were men; not spirit and mind only but body and senses also; and because idealism was not adequate to their need. How solemnly and earnestly is the case presented by the apostle in describing how the human race was brought to the right knowledge of God Himself! "That which was from the beginning, which we have heard, which we have seen with our eyes, which we have looked upon, and our hands have handled, of the Word of Life, that declare we unto you" [1 John 1:1]. God did not reveal Himself to abstract thought; nor is the knowledge of Him and our relation to Him derivable from abstract thought. He came among us, and was seen and heard in the visible form of that human nature in which He dwelt; now we still see Him, in the religion of Sacramentality and Symbolism, which do for us what sight and touch and hearing did for those who were near Him in the days of His flesh.

DIX, *SACRAMENTAL*, 191–92.

A WORLD INSTINCT WITH MYSTERY

An invincible faith in things unseen; a realization of the supernatural realm with its marvelous contents; a constant tending towards God, in holding out the hand for Him, feeling after Him, seeking to be where He is, sure of nothing where He is not discerned, these are the factors of the re-creation in Christ, and these are in vital harmony and accord with the system displayed under holy sacraments and symbols apt to the work of the training of the soul, the renewal of the heart. The Christian dispensation, to judge of it from its description in the Holy Gospels and the New Testament writings, was intended to do a specific work among us. It was designed to act on the heart, to form a peculiar character, . . . and to make him very calm and strong in a strength not his by nature. . . . The result, where the system has its way untrammeled, is that, to the disciple so instructed, the whole world becomes instinct with solemn mysteries and full of things divine; life is, in its experiences, a continual lesson in the dealings of our merciful Lord with us; things about us are more than they seem to be; visible objects stand for invisibles; there are meanings in every department of nature which the natural eye cannot take in; . . . stars and flowers and mountains, rivers, lakes, the ancient hills, the wide and wandering sea, all have, in truth and reality, a voice for the soul; the year has its divisions, the day its hours, through which the mystery of redemption is continually repeated; every duty rests on a law of the God of righteousness, every action should be done to His glory, every work begun, continued, and ended in him.

DIX, *SACRAMENTAL*, 210–12.

BAPTISM AS THE STARTING POINT

First of all, holy Baptism begins Christian training. Without it, whatever other training may be given, Christian training is an impossibility. Christian training differs from all other training in this one respect, that it believes in an implanted supernatural life, which can be and must be developed. It oftentimes uses some of the same means . . . which other training uses, but it uses them to develop a new and a divine life infused into the soul by the Sacrament of the new birth. It trains the child as a member of Christ and a child of God.

DEKOVEN, *SERMONS*, 55.

BAPTISMAL HOPE

The child is baptized once for all into Christ, into His Death; he is once for all made partaker of the benefits of His Death. But during the child's whole life and being afterwards, God graciously means, and we are humbly to pray, that the child may partake of the Resurrection, i.e. of what is sometimes called the Risen Life of our Lord: that as Christ dieth no more, so the baptized may sin no more: that as Christ ascended into Heaven, so we may in heart and mind thither ascend. Thus we ask for each little one the grace of improvement: and we end with asking the grace of final perseverance: "that finally, with the residue of Thy Holy Church, he may be an inheritor of Thine everlasting Kingdom." Thus from the beginning we look on with hope unto the end. We stand in the strait and narrow gate, the lowly baptismal entrance into Christ's Kingdom, and we look along the strait and narrow way, and see the glimmering, more or less clearly, of Eternal Life at the end. We look on in faith and charitable prayer, as St. Paul looked on for his Thessalonians: praying that God would "sanctify them wholly, and preserve their whole spirit and soul and body blameless unto Christ's" aweful "coming" [1 Thess 5:23]. This is our prayer, our hope is steadfast: for we know how faithful He is. He hath called us: He will do it. He for His part is most sure to hear His Church's prayer, and to keep us in the right way.

KEBLE, *VILLAGE SERMONS*, 290.

THE SURE PLEDGE OF BAPTISM

Faith acknowledges in the little child, given back from the Font to the Church's arms, an instance of God's miraculous mercy in raising a soul from death to life: Faith sees in Holy Baptism a lively image of the Death and Burial of Christ, and of His rising again from the dead. To him that believeth, Holy Baptism, especially if it be done by immersion, represents our profession. . . . Just consider this for a moment. First, when you see a child christened, you see things done, which are indeed most simple in themselves, yet, taken altogether, they contain in them very many of the chief truths which we are bound to believe. The three Immersions, or Pourings, with the Threefold Holy Name, represents to us the mystery of the Trinity in Unity: the plunging of the child in the water is like the Death and Burial of Jesus Christ: his rising up again is like Christ's Resurrection: the water represents the sanctifying Power of God's Spirit: the ministering Priest represents Jesus Christ, God and Man, pouring that Good Spirit upon us, or, as St. John Baptist said, baptizing us with the Holy Ghost. Thus does Holy Baptism represent our profession, in respect of what we are to believe of God's saving mercy; and no less does it represent our profession, in respect of what we are to do, that we may not forfeit that mercy. It is an outward and visible sign, both of our blessing and of our duty. It is a sure pledge, whenever we think of it, that we are dead unto sin and risen again unto righteousness: and no less is it a lesson which cannot be mistaken, how we are to lead the rest of our short lives here on earth. It represents unto us, how that we have promised and vowed to follow the example of our Saviour Christ, and, by God's mercy, to be made like unto Him. . . .

KEBLE, *VILLAGE SERMONS*, 302–3.

NEW LIFE IN BAPTISM

God help the man who thinks lightly of that first of the two great sacraments necessary to salvation! It is no empty form, no mere sign to the world, no ceremony which one may decline or pass through without affecting his eternal hopes. On the contrary, it is a mighty agency of the Holy Ghost, always effectual to the ends for which it was instituted, and marking, in each instance, the new birthday of the Christian soul. Now among the ends served by our baptism was this: it was a call from Christ; it was our election into His kingdom; it made us, actually and from that hour, members of Christ and citizens of the New Jerusalem, the city from above. Effectually, whenever a child or any person is baptized, that is done for him which was done for Adam, when God Almighty added to all ordinary natural endowments, the supernatural gifts and graces relating to an immortality of perpetual life and light. Effectually, whenever a child or a person is baptized, his relations to the dying world are changed, and merged into a new condition: the old life is lost, taken away, hidden, buried out of sight.

DIX, *CHRIST AT THE DOOR*, 267.

THE HOLY COMMUNION

In the sacrament of the altar we are brought to the point where the natural and the supernatural come most closely together. To the eye of faith, the Christian Altar appears like a headland jutting into a vast and open sea; waves roll in from the eternal space, to strike upon the shores of time. It is a mirror of all truth, human and divine. It has a twofold aspect, being Sacrifice and Sacrament in one; it is each in turn, in complete and matchless perfection; it is the pure and unbloody Offering, the heavenly Feast. It represents the work of the world's High Priest, now going on above; it brings Him, verily and indeed, into our midst with holy gifts. It is pictorial, it is practical; a grand action is displayed and accompanied, a work of immediate necessity is carried on. As Christ stands at the mercy-seat on high, appearing before His Father as our Mediator and Redeemer, and making intercession for us, so stands the priest as His representative, offering on earth the same oblation which Christ offers in heaven, and sending up the liturgical prayer. Christ promised to feed men with His Flesh and Blood, adding, "Whosoever eateth My Flesh and drinketh My Blood hath everlasting life, and I will raise him up at the last day" [John 6:54]. Here, in Holy Communion, He meets His faithful children for that purpose, and, under forms selected from the natural world, and hallowed and blessed for a supernatural effect, He gives them what He promised. In its double aspect, as sacrifice, as sacrament, this Rite is first in dignity, and, in power, most efficient. Nothing can be set before it, nor can care, pains, or cost be too great in realizing it for all that it is to our devotion and faith. And this, above all, must we be sure to hold, that it is not ourselves who make it what it is; that it is not our subjective act, nor the moral fitness of the recipient, which gives its reality to that sacrament, and effects the Awful Presence of the Lord therein. Our part is to wait for the Holy Ghost till He come; and, when He has blessed and sanctified the oblation, to draw near with faith, and take the Body and the Blood, feeling that God in Christ is all in all, and that it is He who giveth us the bread that feedeth unto everlasting life.

DIX, *SACRAMENTAL*, 148–50.

LESSONS IN LOVE

There are times again, when those who try to be dutiful learners in Christ's school of love, which is His Church, feel themselves, in drawing near to His Sacraments which are most especial lessons of love, more than usually lifted up with loving thankfulness, or cast down with loving contrition, in His gracious Presence. Often they have felt dull and dry, and have gone away, it may be in fear, that they had missed the blessing: but at times it has seemed otherwise, a light has shone in the dark place of their hearts; and whereas before Holy Communion all had seemed more or less dreary, after it, He Whom they had received by faith permitted them to rejoice in His holy comfort; they knew not how, but they could not doubt that it was He. They could not doubt it, when they found themselves afterwards the stronger to resist temptation, and to do good works. This love also was of God, and of God only: who can doubt it? It came not of the outward sign, but of the thing signified, i.e. Christ communicating Himself through that outward sign. If it were slighted, if we fell away, it was, in each instance, a lesson, a divine lesson, in heavenly love, thrown away. . . .

KEBLE, *SERMONS*, 230.

COMMUNION AND COMMERCE

Many of those who are most emphatic upon the Sacramental Presence of Our Lord in the Bread which is His Body and the Wine which is His Blood never seem to have thought out or pondered over the connection between that Presence and the presence of God in His whole creation. That neglect is a disaster to religion. We must be quite clear, that we go to find Him there, so that we may the better find Him everywhere; that the Sacrament leads us, not to a localization, but to a deeper sense of the Omnipresence, of God. The connection between the Sacrament and what is loosely called the "Sacramental Principle" of the universe, needs to be perceived and firmly held. He makes Himself known to us in the Breaking of Bread, that He may more truly and consciously be the honoured guest at every meal, and the most living partner in every enterprise whereby we earn our daily bread. That is why the Collection at the Sacrament becomes the Offertory, and the "alms" are one with the "oblations" —our money being united with the Bread and the Wine, that through His Presence in the Bread and Wine He may consecrate our money to be a spiritual bond of Peace throughout the world. To neglect or put in the background this essential connection is to make sacramental worship quite definitely idolatrous. If Holy Communion does not lead to honest commerce, it fails of its fruit, and "by their fruits ye shall know them" [Matt 7:16]. Commerce is communion, and it must either be Holy Communion, or a cursed counterfeit, which leads not to life but to death. Once and for all let us remember, that the sweep of the Sacrament is as wide as the world. If our faith in the real presence of our Lord in the consecrated Bread upon the altar does not really lead us to perceive His real presence in all bread—if it amounts to anything like the localization of the Presence of God—our sacramental worship has in itself the nature of sin, for sin, at its root, is the denial of the Omnipresence of God. If our love of God's House does not consecrate for us all houses and all homes, if it tends to separate the sanctuary and the street, then our religious observances are literally blasphemous.

STUDDERT KENNEDY, *THE WICKET GATE*, 167–68.

A SACRIFICE OF THANKSGIVING

The eucharist being, as its name imports, a sacrifice of thanksgiving, the bread and wine, after they have been offered or given to God, and blessed and sanctified by his Holy Spirit, are returned by the hand of his minister to be eaten by the faithful, . . . to denote their being at peace and in favour with God, being thus fed at his table, and eating of his food; and also to convey to the worthy receivers all the benefits and blessings of Christ's natural body and blood, which were offered and slain for their redemption.

For this reason, the eucharist is also called the communion of the body and blood of Christ; not only because, by communing together, we declare our mutual love and good will, and our unity in the church and faith of Christ; but also because, in that holy ordinance, we communicate with God through Christ the Mediator, by first offering . . . to him the sacred symbols of the body and blood of his dear Son, and then receiving them again, blessed and sanctified by his Holy Spirit, to feast upon at his table, for the refreshment of our souls; for the increase of our faith and hope; for the pardon of our sins; for the renewing of our minds in holiness, by the operation of the Holy Ghost; and for a principle of immortality to our bodies, as well as to our souls.

From this consideration, the necessity of frequently communicating in the holy eucharist evidently appears. It is the highest act of christian worship; a direct acknowledgment of God's sovereignty and dominion over us, and over all his creatures. It is the memorial of the passion and death of our dear Redeemer, made before the Almighty Father, to render him propitious to us, by pleading with him the meritorious sufferings of his beloved Son, when he made his soul an offering for sin. It is a sensible pledge of God's love to us, who, as he hath given his Son to die for us, so hath he given his precious body and blood, in the holy eucharist, to be our spiritual food and sustenance. And as the bread of this world, frequently taken, is necessary to keep the body in health and vigour, so is this bread of God, frequently received, necessary to preserve the soul in spiritual health, and keep the divine life of faith and holiness from becoming extinct in us.

SEABURY, *DISCOURSES*, 160–61.

AN EXHORTATION

To those who are customary attendants at the Lord's table, we address the exhortation: Take care that your attendance there be not merely the result of habit; let it be dictated by the powerful sentiments of duty, of gratitude, and of love to your God and Saviour. When you present yourselves before him, and become guests at his table, let all your Christian virtues be in lively exercise. While you examine yourselves more or less minutely as circumstances admit, and resolve to resist those temptations to which you may have in some degree yielded, those sins to which you feel you are most liable, and to cherish those Christian dispositions and duties in which you are most deficient, always bear in mind that your strength in this arduous work must be from on high, and that you must come to the Lord's table as sinners, whose trust is not in your own righteousness, but in God's manifold and great mercies and grace. Let your faith be steadily fixed on the great atonement made by the offering of the body and blood which are set forth at the holy table. When you receive the memorials of the love and mercy of him who died for his enemies, sacrifice on his altar all your wrathful passions. When you commemorate the love of him who died for you, return this love by the only tribute in your power—the oblation of yourselves to his service. And realizing the inestimable blessings of pardon, of grace, and of life, which your Saviour, by the death and passion which you commemorate, hath procured for you, gratefully and joyfully participate of the symbols by which these blessings are conveyed and assured.

HOBART, The Posthumous Works, 155–56.

THE COMMEMORATION OF THE CROSS

In the first ages of the Church, the commemoration of the Cross, in its appointed sacrament, was made, at least, on every Lord's day. Ancient piety could not be called too often to remember the death of the atoning Lamb. Ancient faith could not receive too frequently that blessed blood and body, which are the "drink indeed" and "meat indeed" of the immortal soul. And ancient charity, while it felt all its unworthiness of so great mercies, and remembered to what suffering multitudes, lying in darkness and death's shadow, these mercies of redemption were unknown, would not come empty-handed to "such a heavenly feast." Hence, at the administration of the Holy Supper, on the Holy Day, the oblations of the faithful were presented. "Upon the first day of every week," each one of them laid somewhat by itself, according as he had been prospered, putting it into the treasury [1 Cor 16:2]. The sum of all these sacred contributions was "laid at the Apostles' feet; and distribution was made to every man, according as he had need" [Acts 4:35]. While this was so, there was no lack in the Lord's treasury. In the midst of prejudice, against every form of opposition, in spite of utmost persecution by imperial power, the Church went conquering on, till it had filled the world, and bowed the Roman eagle to the Cross.

DOANE, *LIFE AND WRITINGS* 1:451–52.

A PERSONAL RELATIONSHIP

Let us all remember that our religion is the religion of a personal Saviour. It is not a system of ethics, it is not a scheme of philosophy, it is not a conclusion of science, but it is personal love to a personal living Saviour. . . . It is a personal religion, by which we can say, "He loved me, and gave Himself for me"—"The life which I now live in the flesh, I live by the faith of the Son of God, who loved me and gave Himself for me" [Gal 2:20]. And then, in all your experiences, however deep they may be, when you enter the shadow of death, and go through the agony of the dissolution of your body—you can say: "He loved me, and gave Himself for me." He loved me and washed me from my sins in His Blood, to Him be glory and dominion and praise henceforth and for ever, Amen.

STANTON, *LAST SERMONS*, 313.

WHERE TIME AND ETERNITY MEET

Eucharistic people take their lives, and break them, and give them, in daily fulfillment of what our Lord did and does. No need to ask what school of thought you follow or how you speculate about the manner of these things. He took His life in His own hands—this is Freedom. He broke it—this is Obedience. He gave it—this is Love. And He still does these simple acts at every altar and in every heart that will have it so; and Time and Eternity meet. The dying of the Lord Jesus and His life weave the wonderful, humble fabric of Christian discipleship.

BAYNE, *NOW IS THE ACCEPTED TIME*, 23.

THE PRAYING CHURCH

The praying Christian is also part of the praying Church, however solitary he or she may be or feel. The praying Church means not only the local community or the church of a country or a generation, but rather the Holy Catholic Church of Christ, the people of God in all places and ages. Divisions of place and time, of culture, and of our unhappy separations may hinder but they do not destroy the unity in Christ of those who know their prayer to be in the Spirit of Christ. To say this is not to deny the solitude of individual Christians in the uniqueness in which the Creator made them. . . .

The Eucharist is the supreme encounter between God and His redeemed people, through recalling the death of Jesus. Here His people feed upon Jesus, who died and rose again, and offer themselves to the Father in union with his own perfect sacrifice.

RAMSEY, *GLORY DESCENDING*, 45.

LEARNING TO SEE CHRIST

[Another] critical question [I am sometimes asked] is this: "Should we not see Christ's presence everywhere, in the street and in the neighbour, rather than in the Host upon the altar? Are we not imprisoning him in the church?" . . .

Certainly, we must acknowledge that Christ can be encountered anywhere. But I do think that we need a focus where we encounter him face to face if we are to learn to recognize him in other places where he may be hard to discern. Most of us have far too little sensitivity to Christ in the world, and unless we get some training in sensitivity, he may elude us altogether. I could walk around Piccadilly Circus or Times Square for hours, among the garish scenes and the fevered crowds, and, left to myself, I doubt if I would ever have any sense of God or Christ in such places. But if I watch for a little hour in Christ's sacramental presence, exposed to the essence and concentrated fulness of his saving life and death and resurrection, then I hope I shall begin to acquire the kind of sensitivity that will enable me to recognize and respond to Christ in situations where his presence is not obvious.

MACQUARRIE, *PATHS IN SPIRITUALITY*, 35, 37–38.

GRACE TO DO GOOD

The great lesson which man has to learn is that of obedience and submission to God; to be ready to do every thing which God requires, and to forbear every thing which he hath forbidden. And his great duty consists in the exercise of penitence, by which he forsakes sin, and approaches as near as possible to a state of innocency. The foundation of both is faith. . . .

. . . Our very capacity of goodness of every kind we owe to the merciful interposition of our Redeemer. And, in truth, all that we can do toward our own salvation, is not to resist or counteract what God does for us by his Holy Spirit. If we think a good thought, it is by his inspiration. If we have a good wish, it is from his influence. If we do a good action, to him we owe both the intention, and the ability to perform it. "There is none good but one, that is God" [Matt 19:17]. Therefore, every thing that is good must be from God.

Hence appears the necessity of the presence of the Holy Spirit with us; and, of our doing every thing that God directs, in order to obtain it. For this purpose, his holy apostles have instituted the rite of laying on of hands, as one of the first principles of our religion, and require our compliance with it, that we may, by God's mercy, obtain the gifts and graces of his Holy Spirit, by the hands of his authorized minister, in such kind and degree, as he sees best for us. But, it is to be remembered, that in order to obtain the benefits of any ordinance, its observance must be accompanied by those dispositions of heart which are represented or signified by the ordinance. For example, baptism represents and signifies a death unto sin, as well as a new birth unto righteousness. To obtain the new birth unto righteousness, we must therefore come to baptism with true penitence for all our past sins, and with hearty resolution to live in all holiness for the time to come. To apply this to confirmation: The laying on of hands represents and signifies the dominion, protection and guidance of the Holy Spirit. We must, therefore, come to confirmation with a willing disposition to live in subjection to the Spirit of God, to abide ever under his most holy protection, and to follow his heavenly guidance in all things. The same penitence must therefore be necessary in confirmation, that is necessary in baptism; the same firm faith in the promises of God; the same renunciation of every thing that stands in opposition to him; the devil and all his works, the world with its vanities and extravagancies, and all the wicked tempers it produces, and all the evil desires and appetites of the body. It is also evident, that the ordinance requires a hearty desire to be made partakers of the Holy Spirit, and a firm belief that God will give and continue to us his heavenly grace, to preserve us pure and undefiled . . . , to strengthen our good purposes, and enable us to bring them to good effect, by living in obedience to God, to the end of our lives.

SEABURY, *DISCOURSES*, 138–40.

THE CALLING OF A CHRISTIAN

[T]he ordinance of confirmation . . . is calculated to draw . . . attention, at stated periods, to those everlasting concerns which, amidst the occupations and . . . enjoyments of life, are often forgotten or neglected. When a solemn call is made on baptized Christians to assume the engagements by which they were originally entered into covenant with God—when the momentous duties and the high privileges of their calling in Christ Jesus are presented before those who bear his name, and who have been pledged to his service—the appeal is powerfully calculated to excite their serious reflection, to withdraw their attention from the world, and to impress on them the infinite importance of an attention to the things which belong to their eternal peace.

In the solemnity of confirmation, also, those who . . . have assumed the obligations, and received a title to the privileges of their Christian adoption, are reminded of the momentous force of these obligations, and of the exalted nature of these privileges: it is calculated to impress on them their great guilt, as far as they have violated these obligations and contemned these privileges; and in this case also, of the indispensable necessity of their returning unto God, resolving no longer to live in violation of their Christian duties, and in neglect of their Christian privileges. The call, especially on the young members of Christ's fold, to assume their Christian obligations, has a tendency to awaken them to a sense of the supreme importance, above all worldly concerns, of making their Christian calling and election sure.

At the period of the administration of this ordinance, Christian parents and others must feel, in more than its usual force, their awful responsibility for the spiritual welfare of those whom Providence hath placed under their charge—these immortal beings, whose happiness or misery, through a never-ending existence, in no small degree depends on their instruction and care. And at this season also, the ministers and pastors of Christ's fold must be impressed with their accountability for the flock committed to them, and particularly for those young members of it whom they perhaps admitted into this fold at the sacred font, and whom they behold arrived at a season of life when generally the course is taken which leads through the ways of sin and sensuality to the chambers of misery, or through the paths of holiness to the glories of God's kingdom above.

It is a strong sense of this responsibility which excites the earnest solicitude, that all they who have not received the ordinance of confirmation, should embrace the present opportunity of ratifying, in that holy rite, their baptismal engagements, in order that they may have assured to them their baptismal privileges.

HOBART, *THE POSTHUMOUS WORKS*, 88–90.

7

A Pilgrim's Journey

CHRISTMAS

Today the joy of Christmas shines in a world that is darkened by sadness. How real are the gifts of human goodness, nonetheless: they are gifts from the God of Bethlehem who is their source; for God who took human flesh in the stable is God from whose store of love humanity's gifts of love are drawn.

The stable is a symbol of Christ's poverty. The characteristic that gave him the title poor was his *simplicity*. He did without many of the things that people crave for. None did he criticise more severely than those who hankered after more and more possessions and who were preoccupied with money. The worth of a person's life, he insisted, does not consist of possessions, for piling things up does not increase worth. People matter more than things, as people have an eternal destiny. Those who do not fuss about their standard of living and their luxuries are freer to love one another, to serve one another and to enjoy one another. Christ became poor, and he chose the way of simplicity; and if we follow him he promises us riches of his own, riches of happiness and brotherhood shared with one another and with him.

How did Christ become poor? By coming to share in the limitations, frustrations, and hard realities of our human life, our pains and sorrows, and even our death. The imagery of Christ's riches and his poverty is a vivid picture of the Incarnation; but it is another thing to grasp its moral message and to live by it, the message of simplicity and self-sacrifice. Christ gave himself to us to enable us to give ourselves to one another: that is the message of Bethlehem to a world in trouble.

Come to Bethlehem once again: see the stable—see the child. Knowing that he is God made man, knowing that he who was rich has become poor for us, let us kneel in the darkness and cold that is the symbol of our blind and chilly human hearts, and say in a new way: "yours is the kingdom, the power and the glory forever."

RAMSEY, GLORY DESCENDING, 15–16.

PERFECT HUMANITY

The Incarnation . . . the beginning of the earthly life of Christ, was the fulfillment, the filling full, of a human nature by Divinity. We do not ask, we do not dare to hope to know, what was the influence upon Divinity of that mysterious union. But of what was its influence upon humanity there certainly can be no doubt. It made the man in whom the miracle occurred, absolutely perfect man. It did not make Him something else than man. If it had done that, all His value as a pattern for humanity . . . would be gone. Whenever He says to men "Follow Me"; "Be like Me," He is declaring that He is man as they are men, that the peculiar Divinity which filled Him, while it carried humanity to its complete development, had not changed that humanity into something which was no longer human. Can we picture that to ourselves? Is it not just as when the sunlight fills a jewel? The jewel throbs and glows with radiance. All its mysterious nature palpitates and burns with clearness. It opens depths of color which we did not see before. But still it is the jewel's self that we are seeing. The sunlight has made us see what it is, not turned it into something different from what it was. Or to take another illustration which perhaps comes nearer to our truth. A man becomes a scholar. He learns all rich and elevating truth. As that truth enters into him, his human nature opens and deepens and unfolds its qualities. He becomes "more of a man," as we say in one of our common phrases. But that very phrase, "more of a man," implies that he becomes not something different from man, but more truly and completely man. His manhood is not changed into something else; it is developed into a completer self by the truth which he learns.

In both these cases one thing evidently appears; which is that the developing power which brings the being into which it enters to its best has essential and natural relations to the being which it develops. The jewel belongs to the light. The man belongs to the knowledge. And this must always be the truth which must underlie all understanding of the

Incarnation. Man belongs to God. The human nature belongs to the Divine. It can come to its best only by the entrance and possession of it by Divinity. The Incarnation, let us always be sure, was not unnatural and violent but in the highest sense supremely natural. It is the first truth of all our existence that man is eternally the son of God. No man who forgets or denies that truth can really lay hold of the lofty fact that God entered into man.

Brooks, The Candle of the Lord, 255–57.

EPIPHANY

Nothing is more fit than at the time His body was ordained Him, and that is today, to come to the body so ordained.

And in the old Ritual of the Church we find that on the cover of the canister, wherein was the sacrament of His body, there was a star engraven, to shew us that now the star leads us thither, to His body there.

And what shall I say now, but according as St. John saith, and the star, and the wise men say, "Come" [Rev 21:17]. And He, Whose the star is, and to Whom the wise men came, saith "Come." And let them that are disposed, "Come." And let whosoever will, take of the "Bread of Life, which came dow'n from Heaven" [John 6:35, 41] this day into Bethlehem, the house of bread. Of which Bread the Church is this day the house, the true Bethlehem, and all the Bethlehem we have now left to come to for the Bread of life—of that life which we hope for in Heaven. And this our nearest coming that . . . we can come, till we shall by another *venite* come, unto Him in His Heavenly Kingdom. To which He grant we may come, that this day came to us in earth that we thereby might come to Him and remain with Him for ever, "Jesus Christ the Righteous."

Andrewes, Seventeen Sermons on the Nativity, 244.

THE LIGHT OF THE EPIPHANY

This season of Epiphany is the special commemoration of those promises of God, that at last He would bestow on the world the blessing of spiritual light. Out of all the holy days of the year it is the one which reminds us of the light which we have. Other days remind us of what God has done for us. The Epiphany reminds us, not only of what He has done, but of what He has granted us, even here, to know of Himself and of His doings. It is conceivable that He might have done His great works on our behalf without telling us so much. In former generations of the world, He loved men and watched over them, without their knowing it; He prepared good things for them, without letting them into His counsels. We cannot doubt that what Christ has done and suffered concerns, in some way, even those who have never heard His name. But for us, He has put aside, in a degree, the veil which hides from us on earth the presence and working of God, and has admitted us to know what is of the deepest interest to us—partially at least, as they see and know in heaven. This is what we are invited to think of at this time—of this opening of our eyes to God's purposes and presence, this appearing to us of His very self. Things that, in other ages, neither Jew nor Gentile knew of—things that many kings and prophets and righteous men desired to see, and died without seeing—God has made our common heritage. This is our great and real privilege, to know that about ourselves and our relation to God, which we could not have found out, which only in our later ages was made known. Our eyes have seen indeed "the Lord's salvation, which He had prepared before the face of all people; a light to lighten the Gentiles, and the glory of his people Israel" [Luke 2:30–32]. "Through the tender mercy of our God . . . the dayspring from on high hath visited us; to give light to them that sit in darkness and in the shadow of death, to guide our feet into the way of peace" [Luke 1:78–79]. So did the expiring voices of ancient prophecy, on the lips of Simeon and Zacharias, pass into the awakening strains of the Gospel. They express the great truth that we are dealt with henceforth not as children but as men; trusted with the amazing secret of our real destiny; not merely meant for a greatness beyond all we can think or know, but told that we have been meant for it, and told of all that God has done to bring us to it. Today we remember the first steps and stages of that great manifestation, by which we have been brought from darkness to light: and that Light was Christ.

. . . The Epiphany is a sort of figure of the way in which the Light is shown us. The Wise Men came, and looked on the King of the Jews, and worshipped Him, and then they went on their way, and saw Him no more. So it is to us who read their history. They came, we know not whence; they pass before us, beholding, rejoicing in the supreme and ineffable wonder of this our world; they disappear, we know not whither. Such are all the disclosures of Christ's glory. They are here just long enough for men to be certain of them, and to take in what they are; and then the common course of things succeeds, and closes over them.

They come like strangers into the ordinary experience of our present life, with their gracious blessing of illumination, or assurance, or warning, or strength; and having done their work, they leave us and the world to go our way.

So Christ came and went. A little while, in the world's long history, men saw Him, and their hands handled Him, and their ears heard Him; their sick bodies sprang to health under His power, their dead heard His voice and lived. And again, a little while, and they saw Him no more; He came not to stay, but to disclose Himself, and to go; and the world and mankind were left, to the end of time, to remember and to think of the overwhelming manifestation which had once been made to them. So is the light vouchsafed to us here. It is given us but in part, in broken lights. . . . It is given, not to sight, but to remembrance: given us to remember if we will, to forget, also, if we choose: it is the knowledge of heaven, but received on earth, and with the limitations of earth; the knowledge of One, really so near, seemingly so remote, of whom, in our deepest and truest selves we are sure, but whom, in our outer, surface life, we are unable to see, unable to point out, unable fully to prove. For the Infinite Majesty is not *here*; and it is of Him, His Person, His Will, His doings, that the reflections come down into this little life of ours.

CHURCH, *CATHEDRAL AND UNIVERSITY SERMONS*, 80–81, 90–91.

TO WALK WITH CHRIST

Christ was the Son of God. But remember in what sense He ever used this name—Son of God because Son of Man. He claims Sonship in virtue of His Humanity. Now, in the whole previous revelation through the prophets, etc., one thing was implied—only through man can God be known: only through a perfect man, perfectly revealed. Hence He came, "the brightness of His Father's glory, the *express image* of His person" [Heb 1:3]. Christ, then, must be loved as Son of man before He can be adored as Son of God. In personal love and adoration of Christ the Christian religion consists, not in correct morality, or in correct doctrines, but in a homage to the King.

Now, unquestionably, the belief in the Divinity of Christ is waning among us. They who hold it have petrified it into a theological dogma without life or warmth, and thoughtful men are more and more beginning to put it aside. How are we, then, to get back this belief in the Son of God? . . . Begin as the Bible begins, with Christ the Son of Man. Begin with Him as God's character revealed under the limitations of humanity. Lay the foundations of a higher faith deeply in a belief of his Humanity. See Him as He was. Breathe His Spirit. After that, try to comprehend His Life. Enter into his Childhood. Feel with Him when He looked round about Him in anger, when He vindicated the crushed woman from the powerless venom of her ferocious accusers; when He stood alone in time solitary Majesty of Truth in Pilate's judgment-hall; . . . when His heart-strings gave way upon the Cross. Walk with Him through the Marriage Feast. See how the sick and weary came to Him instinctively; how men, when they saw Him, felt their sin, they knew not why, and fell at His feet; how guilt unconsciously revealed itself, and all that was good in men was drawn out, and they became higher than themselves in His presence. Realize this. Live with Him till He becomes a living thought, ever present, and you will find a reverence growing up which compares with nothing else in human feeling. You will feel that a slighting word spoken of him wounds with a dart more sharp than personal insult. You will feel that to bow at the name of Jesus is no form at will of others, but a relief and welcome. . . . For what is it to adore Christ?—to call Him God: to say Lord, Lord? No. Adoration is the mightiest love the soul can give, call it by what name you will.

ROBERTSON, LIVING THOUGHTS, 34–36.

AT GOD'S RIGHT HAND

At God's right hand is not only power, power while we be here to protect us with His might outward, and to support us with His grace inward; but at "His right hand also is the fulness of joy for ever," saith the Psalm [16:11]; joy, and the fulness of joy, and the fulness of it for evermore.

This is meant by His seat at the right hand on the throne. And the same is our blessed **hope** also, that it is not His place only, and none but His, but **even** ours in expectation also. The love of His cross is to us a pledge of the hope of His throne, or whatsoever else He hath or is worth. For if God have given us Christ, and Christ thus given Himself, what hath God or Christ They will deny us? It is the Apostle's own deduction [Rom 8:32].

To put it out of all doubt, hear we His own promise That never brake His word. "To him that overcometh will I give to sit with Me in My throne" [Rev 3:21]. Where to sit is the fulness of our desire, the **end** of our race, *omnia in omnibus*; and farther we cannot go. . . .

Let us now turn to Him and beseech Him, by the sight of this day, by Himself first, and by His cross and throne both—both which He hath set before us, the one to awake our love, the other to quicken our hope— that we may this day and ever lift up our eyes and heads, that we may this day and ever carry them in our eyes and hearts, look up to them both; so look that we may love the one, and wait and hope for the other; so love and so hope that by them both we may move and that swiftly, even run to Him; and running not faint, but so constantly run, that we may fail not finally to attain the happy fruition of Himself, and of the joy and glory of his blessed throne. . . .

ANDREWES, NINETY-SIX SERMONS, 183–84.

GOOD FRIDAY

What are we . . . to think of this day? God in Pain; God sorrowing; God dying for man, as far as God could die. Now it is this; —the blessed news that God suffered pain, God sorrowed, God died, as far as God could die—which makes the Gospel different from all other religions in the world; and it is this, too, which makes the Gospel so strong to conquer men's hearts, and soften them, and bring them back to God and righteousness in a way no other religion ever has done. It is the good news of this good day, well called Good Friday, which wins souls to Christ, and will win them as long as men are men. . . .

Good Friday showed that there was sympathy, there was fellow-feeling between God and man; that God would do all for man, endure all for man; that God so desired to make man like God, that he would stoop to be made like man. There was nothing God would not do to justify himself to man, to show men that he did care for them, that he did love the creatures whom he had made. Yes; God had not forgotten man; God had not made man in vain. God had not sent man into the world to be wicked and miserable here, and to perish for ever hereafter. Wickedness and misery were here; but God had not put them here, and he would not leave them here. He would conquer them by enduring them. Sin and misery tormented men; then they should torment the Son of God too. Sin and misery killed men; then they should kill the Son of God, too: he would taste death for every man, that men might live by him. He would be made perfect by sufferings: not made perfectly good (for that he was already), but perfectly able to feel for men, to understand them, to help them; because he had been tempted in all things like as they.

And so on Good Friday did God bridge over the gulf between God and men. No man can say now, Why has God sent man into the world to be miserable, while he is happy? For God in Christ was miserable once. No man can say, God makes me go through pain, and torture, and death, while he goes through none of such things; for God in Christ endured pain, torture, death, to the uttermost. And so God is a being which man can love, admire, have fellow-feeling for; cling to God with all the noble feelings of his heart, with admiration, gratitude, and tenderness, even on this day with pity. As Christ himself said, "When I am lifted up, I will draw all men to me" [John 12:32].

KINGSLEY, THE GOOD NEWS OF GOD, 332, 335–36.

THE POWER OF THE RESURRECTION

Today perhaps more than ever before, it is being insisted that Christianity is not doctrine but life; but by life is usually meant not life at all, but a certain ethical habit of action, a certain obedience to moral ideals in our social relations. This has no resemblance at all to what the Christian Scriptures mean by life. By life they mean a new vitality which is the outcome of being put into living union with the humanity of the Risen Jesus, conceived as the medium through which the life of God flows out to the life of men. The life which the Apostles taught depends on the present existence of the Incarnate Redeemer, and our contact with him—our being in him. "In Christ" is the most characteristic phrase of the Apostolic teaching; and by "in Christ" they mean a literal incorporation into the Incarnate Body which takes into its unity each soul that is regenerated in Christ Jesus. . . .

If your religion is to be a living thing, there must come a time when you pass from the acceptance of the truths you have learned to the personal possession of them in a vital experience. This may happen suddenly or it may happen slowly—the important thing is that it happens, and that in the happening you realize yourself as a sinner redeemed by the Blood of Christ and now alive by his life. The birth of personal religion, the religion of experience, as contrasted with the religion of habit, is as needful to-day as any form of conversion was in the early ages of the Church. . . . [T]he reason that to-day we so little find the joy of religion is because we have not passed from passive acceptance of truths we have heard to the active experience of them as power in life. As we look out on Christendom to-day, is not the thing that is conspicuously lacking, just the sense of Christianity as power? We conceive it as decency of conduct, to a certain degree as obligation, perhaps even as privilege; but do we conceive it as power, as driving force, as a new energy which makes life vivid with its activity? Is our Christian life a life swept along by the power of the Resurrection? Do we feel that the love of Christ constraineth us? Is the conviction present to us that just because we are Christians we are not tamely to acquiesce in the conventions of society, but to build up a life-experience that is based on quite other ideals?

BARRY, *MEDITATIONS ON THE APOSTLES' CREED*, 313–14, 323–24.

EASTER FAITH

Easter says to us: have faith! Faith does not mean that we first try to see things in a coherent and intelligible shape and then conclude that God is true. Faith is more like when the women came to the tomb while it was still very dark, and they wondered who could move away the stone as it was very heavy: and look—the stone is gone! When things are very dark, when human possibilities are exhausted, when we are at the end of our tether, God acts. Easter defines for all time the character of Christian faith: human weakness, divine power; I can't, God can; I am weak, God is strong; I am a sinner, God forgives. Does this sound fanciful? It was such a faith that enabled the apostles to carry the gospel into a hostile world. It was such a faith that sustained Christian men and women again and again throughout the centuries. It is like a coin that is always on one side—frailty, penitence, death, and on the other side—power, forgiveness and life. Let the words of St John sound in our hearts today: "This is the victory that overcomes the world—our faith" [1 John 5:4–5].

RAMSEY, *GLORY DESCENDING*, 57–58.

CHRIST'S ASCENSION

And Christ our Master went up on high out of our sight to draw our hearts after him. . . . [T]o Him we owe our supreme loyalty, and duty, and devotion, and boundless trust, as to our Lord and our God. The love of him, the union in affection and will with Him—that is what we profess; that, when it is in reality and truth, is Christian religion.

CHURCH, *CATHEDRAL AND UNIVERSITY SERMONS*, 155–56.

BEYOND THE EARTH

I cannot trace it, but that body of Christ yet lives somewhere in some mysterious and unknown region of this vast creation in one little corner of which we live. Humanity, then, so the Ascension tells me, may be at home somewhere else than on the earth. It has nobler kinships than with the brutes. It may enter into the welcome of larger hospitality than any that the stateliest mountains or forests can extend. The Resurrection had shown that humanity might relive here upon the earth, even after the catastrophe of death, that seems so terribly the end of all. The Ascension showed that out beyond the earth, wherever the vast system of existence is held as a unit in the hand of one Creator who is Lord of all, out to the end of all things over which God reigns, this humanity, which seems to be shut in to one small planet, may go and find a home and kindred beyond the farthest star.

Is that a gain? If every enlargement of the general life of the race is a boon to the weakest and poorest being who bears the human nature and who comes in sight of the larger outlook of his kind, then surely this great light thrown on the range of human existence is indeed a gain to any poor, depressed, and struggling man who comes to believe it. The slave learns that the master who is to him like a god is a man like himself. A humanity like his own sits in those stately halls and walks over those broad fields. A struggling student learns that his humanity has risen to the height of David's song or Newton's insight. A country boy becomes aware of the stupendous distances to which men like himself have explored the globe, and of the strange transcendent regions in which they have planted their human homes. A self-respect, a noble ambition, a consciousness of freedom and of chance, must come. A great, vague, but strong call must sound out of the distance. This dream of being something must gather into a vision and the soul leap into the heaven of new hopes.

BROOKS, *SERMONS*, 296–97.

PENTECOST

We know the power which new and great ideas have in giving a fresh start to the life of men, in remoulding it, and redirecting its course. The promise, the gift of the Holy Ghost, as it shapes and colours the whole language of the New Testament, is such a great idea. . . . However vaguely held, however imperfectly grasped, the belief that there was such a com-

munication between God and the soul of man, that this was the fruit .
. . of the Lord's Ascension, must have of itself awakened men from the
routine of custom, and opened to them new prospects of the possibilities
of improvement. But the gift of the Spirit was not merely an idea, it was a
real power from the unseen world—the very power and working of God.
It was the coming of a Divine Person, one with the Father and the Son,
into these very souls of ours, to work in them His most incomprehen-
sible, but most certain and blessed work. It was something more than the
disclosure of truth, the communication of light and of holy influences
drawing and governing the heart. That which was the special promise of
our Lord before He suffered, that which He solemnly guaranteed after
His Resurrection, that which He sent down and shed abroad after His
Ascension, was no less than a sacred, permanent, indwelling in human
souls, of One who was God with Himself, continually to guide and teach
them; day by day to restore and purify them; at last to fashion them into
the likeness of the Son of God, and to fit them for the eternal and perfect
life. Here in the very centre of our being, in the centre of our wills and
affections, here where we love, and desire, and choose, and act, where
we are tempted, where we conquer, where we sin—here is One who does
more for men than the great Master could do for His disciples when He
was with them; One, who makes known to us all that Christ really is, all
that Christ really means; a Comforter, an Advocate, who is to abide with
us for ever; One, whose presence brings with it holiness, and divine love,
and peace, in a way in which they never were in human souls before;
One, under whose guidance we are going through our discipline, and
learning to shape and present our prayers; One, who knows our deepest
and most inmost needs, and deigns to associate Himself in wonderful,
unspeakable, sympathy with our yearning supplications; One, who in the
awful words of Holy Scripture, makes us one in union with the Father
and the Son; One, whose presence with our spirit, is the pledge to us,
while still in the flesh, of the still greater gifts which our Father reserves
for us in the world where sin and death are not.

Church, *Cathedral and University Sermons*, 171–73.

TRINITY

There are those who incline to sneer at the Trinitarian; those to whom
the doctrine appears merely a contradiction, a puzzle, an entangled,
labyrinthine enigma, in which there is no meaning whatever. But let all

such remember that though the doctrine may appear to them absurd, because they have not the proper conception of it, some of the profoundest thinkers, and some of the holiest spirits among mankind, have believed in this doctrine—have clung to it as a matter of life or death. Let them be assured of this, that whether the doctrine be true or false, it is not necessarily a doctrine self-contradictory. Let them be assured of this, in all modesty, that such men never could have held it unless there was latent in the doctrine a deep truth, perchance the truth of God.

We will take any material substance: we find in that substance qualities; we will say three qualities—color, shape, and size. Color is not shape, shape is not size, size is not color. There are three distinct essences, three distinct qualities, and yet they all form one unity, one single conception, one idea—the idea, for example, of a tree.

Now we will ascend from that into the immaterial world; and here we come to something more distinct still. Hitherto we have had but three qualities: we now come to the mind of man,—where we find something more than qualities. We will take three—the will, the affections, and thoughts of man. His will is not his affections, neither are his affections his thoughts; and it would be imperfect and incomplete to say that these are mere qualities in the man. They are separate consciousnesses, living consciousnesses, as distinct and as really sundered as it is possible for three things to be, yet bound together by one unity of consciousness. Now we have distincter proof than even this that these things are three. The anatomist can tell you that the localities of these powers are different. He can point out the seat of the nerve of sensation; he can localize the feeling of affection; he can point to a nerve and say, "There resides the locality of thought."

There are three distinct localities for three distinct qualities, personalities, consciousnesses; yet all these three are one.

Once more: we will give proof even beyond all that. The act that a man does is done by one particular part of that man. You may say it was a work of his genius, or of his fancy; it may have been a manifestation of his love, or an exhibition of his courage; yet that work was the work of the whole man: his courage, his intellect, his habits of perseverance, all helped toward the completion of that single work. Just in this way certain special works are attributed to certain personalities of the Deity; the work of redemption being attributed to one, the work of sanctification to another. And yet just as the whole man was engaged in doing that work, so does the whole Deity perform that work which is attributed to one essential.

ROBERTSON, *LIVING THOUGHTS*, 222–23.

BELIEF IN THE HOLY SPIRIT

Our belief in the Holy Ghost is belief in a Person who is God and who from all eternity has been God; not created, not begotten, but proceeding from the Father and the Son, the Third Person of the Adorable and Ever-Blessed Trinity. It is belief that this Person who is Lord and Life-Giver works and has worked in the world as creative and constructive power, both in the realm of the natural and of the spiritual, being in both the principle of order, of life and of illumination. It is belief that we, through our incorporation into the Body of Christ, are, in a way that was impossible before the Incarnation, brought into relation to the life of God the Holy Trinity, and are become subject to the action of the Holy Spirit who has become to us an immediate source of inspiration and energy. Our souls are cleansed and stimulated by him, our minds are illumined, our consciences are directed, and our very bodies are become his temples. He interprets the mind of God to us.

BARRY, *MEDITATIONS ON THE APOSTLES' CREED*, 405–6.

THE GUIDANCE OF THE HOLY SPIRIT

The Christian needs a certain self-reliance, which yet is not self-reliance, but reliance upon the fact that he is in Christ and Christ in him, and that his soul is the abode of the Spirit of truth and guidance. We need a certain robustness of faith that will counteract any tendency to morbidity. It is usually morbidity and scrupulosity, with symptoms of spiritual infirmity, which makes people substitute an exterior conscience for the conscience God has given them, and insist upon having their mind and conscience made up for them rather than, in trust in the Presence that is within them, making them up for themselves. It is better for us to make mistakes in good faith, and after earnest thought and prayer, than to avoid mistakes, if we can so avoid them, by a method that leaves us spiritual parasites and weaklings. I recognize fully that there is such a thing as legitimate direction; that there are times when we need exterior help and guidance; that such help and guidance, too, is one of the instruments of the Holy Spirit. But what we need is help and guidance, not the substitution of another will and conscience for our own. For the most part what leads people to seek guidance is not ignorance, but a feeble will that shrinks from meeting duty, and a timorous faith that is afraid to trust itself to God. Sometimes, too, it is a foolish desire to talk about oneself, which is quite one of the lower forms of pride. . . .

I do not believe that the Holy Spirit leaves any one without guidance who throws himself upon him in a spirit of faith and self-surrendered will. I think that we can all look back into our lives and see there times of crisis when important decisions had to be made. We can see now the spirit in which we made them; we can see whether we took them to our Lord and asked his help and the guidance of the Holy Spirit; whether we made them the intention of our communions and fought them to a decision on our knees; or whether we made our decision in a purely worldly spirit and upon considerations of expediency. If the former was our course, I do not believe that we shall find any case in which we have since seen reason to regret our decision. We have again and again verified in our experience God's promise that we shall be taught of him. It may . . . have been true, that when we made our decision we were not altogether clear in our own minds, and were only certain that we were acting for what seemed the best. But the future demonstrated the wisdom of our choice, and that it was the choice of a soul that sought God and was taught of him.

BARRY, *MEDITATIONS ON THE APOSTLES' CREED*, 417–19.

THE GIFT OF THE SPIRIT

Consider . . . that the gift of the Spirit was not a temporary one for the supply of the necessities of the Apostles. The gift of the Spirit is a perpetual gift to the whole Church. He came as the Spirit of guidance to lead the Church into all truth. This work was not accomplished once for all in the direction given to Apostolic lives. The Church has to be guided into the truth in each generation, guided to the solution of the new questions that each generation presents. There will never he an end of the need of the Spirit's guidance till the end of the Kingdom come. And a part of that guidance is the guidance of the individual Christian to the appropriation and use of so much of the truth as is sufficient for his needs. We expect not only that the Church will be guided to meet successfully the problems raised in the course of its attempt to conquer the world for Christ; but we expect that our own individual problems will find their solution through the presence in us of the same Spirit. Indeed, as the Church cannot do its work apart from us, its work is, in a way, dependent upon our response to the impulses of the Spirit. We need, then, ever to be seeking the guidance of the Spirit in the intimate details of our own lives; to review those lives constantly in the light of his inspired teaching; to seek through his guidance to find the mind of Christ; to review in the interior light of his leading all our thoughts and actions, doing nothing except it first be submitted to him. To be led of the Spirit is the aspiration of the Christian's life.

BARRY, *MEDITATIONS ON THE APOSTLES' CREED*, 404–5.

THE TRINITY AND NATURE

God is above nature, but He is also within it. Nature's laws express His mind. Such laws are only limits of God so far as they express that law of perfect reason which is the law of His own mind. . . .

The common tendency is to see God in portents rather than in order and law: His omnipotence has seemed to mean that He can do anything anyhow. But the best theology has held that God has always acted and still acts by law and method. No one can reveal His mind without revealing something of His inner self. Thus, in revealing God, our Lord gave insight into His inner being: this the Church expressed in her doctrine of the Trinity. He did not expressly reveal the doctrine. In their gradual intercourse His disciples recognised Father, Son, and Holy Ghost as included in their thought of God. The process cannot be described; but at last, without doubt of the divine unity, they included in their thought of it the Three Persons. So, too, did the baptismal formula include them in the name of one God. . . . When the Church defined the doctrine, she acknowledged freely that all human words are inadequate to describe the inscrutable being of God. She only wished to guard her trust of truth.

This doctrine of the Trinity is not discoverable by reason, but agreeable to reason. God, we believe, is an eternal and spiritual being. The life of spirit is made up of will, reason, and love. If God is eternal love, there must be an eternal object of His love. A life of reason demands an object of thought; an eternal mind demands an eternal object of thought. Will must issue in product: an eternal will in an eternally sufficient product. Reason tells us that God cannot be a monotonous unity, but must thus contain within Himself distinctions.

There are of course other views of God. Pantheism is one. It gives noble expression to God's presence in all things; but it knows not immortality, nor sin, nor sin's remedy. Mere Deism distinguishes God from the world, but leaves Him in blank solitude, with nothing to answer to His love, His reason, or His will. Christian theology harmonises the two. God is in all things present; but He does not depend upon the world: He exists, too, in Himself, with the Word and the Spirit eternally dwelling in His bosom. God is nature's life, but also its Creator, its Lord, its Judge.

So the Christian worships God behind nature's veil, yet the eternal God. He sees all things in God: that is worship. The human world is like a restless sea, but there is purpose in it. All things move to the divine event. Unity, subordination, worship is the goal of all things.

GORE, *WHY WE CHRISTIANS BELIEVE*, 42–45.

NURSERY GARDENS FOR GOD

The choicest saints have grown up in the darkest times, and from the most unlikely corners of the earth, surrounded by unsympathizing friends, despised and made light of by the world, and have gone on simply doing his or her work in the way God appointed for them, without sympathy or encouragement. They have grown up without reputation for being good, quite neglected, without any one knowing anything about them. So it was here. Out of a despised land, out of a dry ground, our Blessed Saviour grew up like a tender plant before God.

Brethren, I do not know if there is much of this sort of thing among you now, but I know it used to be so, and more or less it is so in all ages. There are solitary lives, growing up like tender plants before God, longing after higher things, despised by the world around. Let such take heart. They are growing like roots out of a dry ground. Most tender plants come out of ground most unlikely to nourish them. Do not give way for an instant to the temptation to despair of following the high calling which God has given you. . . . And God is able to open the hearts of others by His grace, and to help them in the same way. Let no one say "I have no one to help me. No one else cares for this sort of thing. My surroundings are not helpful. I get no help from my friends—*this* is not the ground to produce a saint, it is so very dry!" Be it so. God likes to show His power in that very way, and I cannot help dwelling upon this. Places most unnoticed, uncared for by the world, are the choicest nursery gardens for God.

KING, *DUTY AND CONSCIENCE*, 42–43.

IN THE COMPANY OF THE SAINTS

Every good path which is revealed to us by Christ bears the steps of many who, before us, have walked with Him. Our delight must be, not merely to think of abstract goodness, nor merely to struggle onward with a sense of isolation, where Christ calls. We are not called to follow Him alone. "It is not good for man to be alone" [Gen 2:18]. Christ has provided for one of the deepest needs of our nature, in that He calls us to follow Himself in the communion of saints. We are thus continually to reflect upon the earthly life of the righteous, whose paths we are to keep, and upon the reward of their toil into which they are now entered, and upon the consummation of all things, when we and they shall rejoice together. The life of faith loses a great part of its vigour if we omit the thought of that sympathy whereby the members of Christ in heaven and earth are for ever united.

BENSON, WISDOM, 62–63.

SPORTSMEN AND SAINTS

There is much of kinship between the sportsman and the saint. Both are gamblers, who bet their lives upon a great chance. To the true sports- man, life is a great game and he bets his brain, muscle, and blood, if need be, that his side will win; and a saint is one who plays the game on its highest level, with God for his leader and righteousness for his cause, and everything he possesses for the stakes. The two ideals are not incom- patible, but complementary. It is right that we should take life as a great game, but utterly wrong that we should imagine that games are life. That is just one of many idolatries. Football is the most popular religion in England today; but it will not save us either in body or in soul. We need a bigger game and higher stakes. Gambling, like all vices, is the perver- sion of a virtue; and the sportsmen of the lower level, who hang about our street corners buying up the sporting editions, are perverted saints, betting their pitiful poverty upon petty issues, for the sake of passing excitement—instead of staking all the wealth and the glory of life to at- tain a great and lasting achievement. . . .

We need God to make our sportsmen saints, and our would-be saints into real sportsmen, who know life to be a glorious battle with the chance of everlasting victory, and who go to it with the cry of the Good

Soldier on their lips, "Lead us not into temptation, but deliver us from evil." Of such is the Kingdom of Heaven.

STUDDERT KENNEDY, *THE WICKET GATE*, 228–29.

THE FELLOWSHIP OF THE SAINTS

The Communion or Fellowship of the Saints is a fact which cannot be doubted by anyone who has pondered the change which Christ our Saviour has accomplished in us. However we may express it, the kernel of Christian experience is what S. Paul expresses by his repeated phrase "In Christ." To problem after problem he applies the same solution. We are in Christ; He has taken possession of us so completely that whatever is true of Him is true of us also. Has He suffered the death-penalty due to sin? Then so have we. Has He risen from that death to life indissoluble? Then so have we. Is He enthroned in the heavenly sphere? Then so are we. We do not have to win our ascent from earth to heaven; it has been won for us. Our citizenship is in heaven—now. Our part is not to find the way there, but being there to live worthily of our station.

It is "in Christ" that we have fellowship or Communion with all the Saints of God. For such fellowship, at least in a limited form of it, almost all men crave. The desire for immortality does not chiefly spring from a longing for our own individual continuance; it springs rather from a desire to be assured that the friends who are gone from us are not lost irrevocably, and that one day the old intercourse will be renewed. . . .

Our fellowship with the blessed dead is . . . to be won . . . by our ascent to them, as in the Eucharist we lift up our hearts to the Lord and forthwith it is with Angels and Archangels and with all the company of Heaven that we laud and magnify God's glorious Name. It is in worship and in work that we are one with them. They with us are members of the one great fellowship, the Fellowship or Communion of Saints. The hallowing of God's Name, the coming of His Kingdom, the doing of His will, are still their chief concern; as in prayer and effort we labour for these things we are helping to accomplish what is the chief desire of their hearts.

But we want to come nearer to them than that if we can; and still it must be by prayer. Let us pray for those whom we know and love who have passed on to the other life. . . .

But do not be content to pray for them. Let us also ask them to pray for us. In such prayers while they lived on earth they both displayed and consecrated their love towards us. Doubtless that ministry of love continues; but let us seek it, ask for it, claim it. It is in the mutual service of prayer, our prayer for them and theirs for us, that we come closest to them. For our fellowship with them is "in Christ," and we find them when we seek them in His Name.

We claim the station Christ has won for us. With Him we are conquerors of death and citizens of the eternal world. We seek the saints and our own departed friends in His presence; we are near them when we keep close to Him. He is the Way both to the Father and to the Father's home where His children are gathered.

TEMPLE, *FELLOWSHIP WITH GOD*, 71–72, 77–80.

THE LIVING PAST

The deepest significance of the past is that it contains reflections of what is eternal. Saintly men and women of any age belong to more than their own era: they transcend it. Therefore openness to heaven is necessary for a Christian. Heaven is the final meaning of human beings created in God's own image for lasting fellowship with Him. Openness to heaven is realized in the communion of saints in deliberate acts of prayer and worship. But it is realized no less in every act of selflessness, humility or compassion: for such acts are already anticipations of heaven in the here and now.

RAMSEY, *GLORY DESCENDING*, 132.

8

Vice and Virtue

THE HOURLY OCCASIONS

Vanity is at the bottom of almost all, may we not say, of all our sins? We think more of signalizing than of saving ourselves. We overlook the hourly occasions which occur of serving, of obliging, of comforting those around us, while we sometimes, not unwillingly perform an act of notorious generosity. The habit however in the former case better indicates the disposition and bent of the mind, than the solitary act of splendor. The Apostle does not say whatsoever *great* things ye do, but "whatsoever things ye do, do *all* to the glory of God."

MORE, *PRACTICAL PIETY*, 132.

ORDINARY ACTIONS AND OCCASIONAL PRAYERS

As sure therefore as there is any wisdom in praying for the Spirit of God, so sure is it that we are to make that Spirit the rule of all our actions; as sure as it is our duty to look wholly unto God in our prayers, so sure is it that it is our duty to live wholly unto God in our lives. But we can no more be said to live unto God unless we live unto Him in all the ordinary actions of our life, unless He be the rule and measure of all our ways, than we can be said to pray unto God unless our prayer look wholly unto Him. So that unreasonable and absurd ways of life, whether in labor or diversion, whether they consume our time or our money, are like unreasonable and absurd prayers and are as truly an offence unto God.

. . . You see [many people] strict as to some times and places of devotion, but when the service of the church is over, they are but like those that seldom or never come there. In their way of life, their manner of spending their time and money, in their cares and fears, in their pleasures and indulgences, in their labor and diversions, they are like the rest of the world. This makes the loose part of the world generally make a jest of those that are devout because they see their devotion goes no further than their prayers, and that when they are over they live no more unto God till the time of prayer returns again, but live by the same humour and fancy and in as full an enjoyment of all the follies of life as other people. This is the reason why they are the jest and scorn of careless and worldly people, not because they are really devoted to God, but because they appear to have no other devotion but that of occasional prayers.

LAW, *A SERIOUS CALL*, 26–27.

SELF-AWARENESS

Screwtape to Wormwood:

One can therefore formulate the general rule: In all activities of mind which favour our [Satan's] cause, encourage the patient to be un-selfconscious and to concentrate on the object, but in all activities favourable to the Enemy [God] bend his mind back on itself. Let an insult or a woman's body so fix his attention outward that he does not reflect "I am now entering into the state called Anger—or the state called Lust." Contrariwise let the reflection "My feelings are now growing more devout, or more charitable," so fix his attentions inward that he no longer looks beyond himself to see our Enemy or his own neighbours.

LEWIS, *THE SCREWTAPE LETTERS*, 29–30.

VIRTUE AND VICE

We should cultivate most assiduously, because the work is so difficult, those graces which are most opposite to our natural temper; the value of our good qualities depending much on their being produced by the victory over some natural wrong propensity. The implantation of a virtue is the eradication of a vice. It will cost one man more to keep down a rising passion than to do a brilliant deed. It will try another more to keep back a sparkling but corrupt thought, which his wit had suggested but which his religion checks, than it would to give a large sum in charity.

MORE, *PRACTICAL PIETY*, 30.

CLEVERNESS

. . . [C]leverness is a great temptation to vanity. The single remarks strike persons, and they admire them. Some smile shows it; and the person goes his way and is self-satisfied and his vanity is nourished. . . .

Now just watch yourself for the little occasions in which you think yourself cleverer than another. Perhaps you won't call it clever, but something more solid; a true perception of things. Set yourself against any supposed superiority to any one. One grain of love is better than a hundredweight of intellect. And after all, that blasted spirit, Satan, has more intellect than the whole human race.

PUSEY, *SPIRITUAL LETTERS*, 105.

LUST AND DISILLUSIONMENT

About the sin called *Luxuria* or *Lust*, I shall . . . say only three things. First, that it is a sin, and that it ought to be called plainly by its own name, and neither huddled away under a generic term like immorality, nor confused with love.

Secondly, that up till now the Church, in hunting down this sin, has had the active alliance of Caesar, who has been concerned to maintain family solidarity and the orderly devolution of property in the interests of the State. But now that contract and not status is held to be the basis of society, Caesar need no longer rely on the family to maintain social solidarity; and now that so much property is held anonymously by trusts and joint-stock companies, the laws of inheritance lose a great deal of their importance. Consequently, Caesar is now much less interested than he was in the sleeping arrangements of his citizens, and has in this matter cynically denounced his alliance with the Church. This is a warning against putting one's trust in any child of man—particularly Caesar. If the Church is to continue her campaign against Lust, she must do so on her own—that is, on sacramental—grounds; and she will have to do it, if not in defiance of Caesar, at least without his assistance.

Thirdly, there are two main reasons for which people fall into the sin of Luxuria. It may be through sheer exuberance of animal spirits: in which case a sharp application of the curb may be all that is needed to bring the body into subjection and remind it of its proper place in the scheme of man's twofold nature. Or—and this commonly happens in periods of disillusionment like our own, when philosophies are bankrupt and life appears without hope—men and women may turn to lust in sheer boredom and discontent, trying to find in it some stimulus which is not provided by the drab discomfort of the mental and physical surroundings. When that is the case, stern rebukes and restrictions are worse than useless. It is as though one were to endeavour to cure anaemia by bleeding: it only reduces further an already impoverished vitality. The mournful and medical aspect of twentieth-century pornography and promiscuity strongly suggests that we have reached one of these periods of spiritual depression, where people go to bed because they have nothing better to do. In other words, the "regrettable moral laxity" of which respectable people complain may have its root cause not in Luxuria at all, but in some other of the sins of society, and may automatically begin to cure itself when that root cause is removed.

SAYERS, *CREED OR CHAOS?*, 63–64.

THE DESIRES THAT DISTURB HUMAN LIFE

The man of pride has a thousand wants which only his own pride has created, and these render him as full of trouble as if God had created him with a thousand appetites without creating anything that was proper to satisfy them. Envy and ambition have also their endless wants which disquiet the souls of men, and by their contradictory motions render them as foolishly miserable as those that want to fly and creep at the same time. . . .

For all the wants which disturb human life, which make us uneasy to ourselves, quarrelsome with others, and unthankful to God, which weary us in vain labors and foolish anxieties, which carry us from project to project, from place to place in a poor pursuit of we don't know what, are the wants which neither God, nor nature, nor reason hath subjected us to, but are solely infused into us by pride, envy, ambition, and covetousness.

LAW, *A SERIOUS CALL*, 131, 134.

LIFE AT THE TOP

A Christian lives at the height of his being, not only at the top of his spiritual, but of his intellectual life. He alone lives in the full exercise of his rational powers. Religion ennobles his reason while it enlarges it.

Let, then, your soul act up to its high destination; let not that which was made to soar to heaven, grovel in the dust. Let it not live so much below itself. You wonder it is not more fixed, when it is perpetually resting on things which are not fixed themselves. In the rest of a Christian there is a stability. Nothing can shake his confidence but sin. Outward attacks and troubles rather fix than unsettle him, as tempests from without only serve to root the oak faster, while an inward canker will gradually rot and decay it.

MORE. *PRACTICAL PIETY*, 48.

ENJOYING CREATION

Screwtape to Wormwood:

I would make it a rule to eradicate from my patient any strong personal taste which is not actually a sin, even if it is something quite trivial such as a fondness for county cricket or collecting stamps or drinking cocoa. Such things, I grant you, have nothing of virtue in them; but there is a sort of innocence and humility and self-forgetfulness about them which I distrust. The man who truly and disinterestedly enjoys any one thing in the world, for its own sake, and without caring twopence what other people say about it, is by that very fact forearmed against some of our [Satan's] subtlest modes of attack.

LEWIS, *THE SCREWTAPE LETTERS*, 60.

EVIL SURMISINGS

A suspicious temper is inconsistent with the spirit of Christian charity. *Charity thinketh no evil*, until constrained by forcible testimony. *Charity hopeth all things*; hopeth all things favourable of others, so long as there remains rational ground for hope. *Charity believeth all things*: believeth all things which kindness would incline us to deem credible, and which experience or evidence will permit us to credit. In our opinions, no less than in our actions, let us study, through the influence of divine grace, to be uniformly governed by the law of Christ. Let us do unto others as we might reasonably wish them to do unto us: and think of them as we might reasonably desire that they should think concerning us; and thus, in thought as well as in deed, love our neighbour as ourselves. Where would then be our *evil surmisings*? *Follow after charity.*

GISBORNE, *SERMONS*, 352.

A VITAL EXISTENCE

How is it we suffer people to imagine that goodness is not interesting, nor holiness attractive? How is it that we have not moving about us those saints who would so lightly shatter those fond imaginations? Is it that our type of excellence is so meagre and petty and repressed? Goodness, if it be true goodness, must mean an exhibition of heightened energy. Sin is always sickness, and sickness cannot but be depressing, uncomfortable, impotent, and poor, and whenever it is not this it is only because some goodness is at work within it stronger than the sin. It is not, it is true, sin because it is unpleasant—God forbid!—but it cannot but be unpleasant if it be sin. Goodness is always soundness, and we must not endure to be contented with any standard of goodness which does not give proof of its health; and this it does only when it is cheerful, vigorous, elastic, free, hearty, hopeful, springing, gracious, delightful, beautiful, and strong.

. . . [T]he tendency of our life must be towards health, and therefore towards a more energetic and exhilarating existence. Holiness, in the sense of St. Paul, is always a freeing of the soul from impotence, the setting loose of spiritual energies, of vitalised activities. Is that what it means to us? Have we found it . . . to be a way of increase, of enrichment, of growth, of vigour, of exultation?

HOLLAND, *HELPS*, 110–11.

INCENTIVES TO VIRTUE

It may be laid down as an axiom, that it is more easy to take away superfluities than to supply defects; and, therefore, he that is culpable, because he has passed the middle point of virtue, is always accounted a fairer object of hope, than he who fails by falling short. The one has all that perfection requires, and more, but the excess may be easily retrenched; the other wants the qualities to excellence, and who can tell how he shall obtain them? We are certain that the horse may be taught to keep pace with his fellow, whose fault is that he leaves them behind. We know that a few strokes of the axe will lop a cedar; but what arts of cultivation can elevate a shrub?

. . . False hopes and false terrors are equally to be avoided. Every man, who proposes to grow eminent by learning, should carry in his mind, at once, the difficulty of excellence, and the force of industry; and remember that fame is not conferred but as the recompense of labour, and that labour, vigorously continued, has not often failed of its reward.

JOHNSON, *THE RAMBLER* (NO. 25), 50–51.

THE STATE OF MORAL VIRTUE

Among the sentiments which almost every man changes as he advances into years, is the expectation of uniformity of character. He that without acquaintance with the power of desire, the cogency of distress, [or] the complications of affairs . . . has filled his mind with the excellence of virtue, and having never tried his resolution in any encounters with hope or fear, believes it able to stand firm whatever shall oppose it, will be always clamorous against the smallest failure . . . and . . . consider every man that fails in any part of his duty, as without conscience and without merit; unworthy of trust, or love, of pity, or regard; as an enemy whom all should join to drive out of society, as a pest which all should avoid, or as a weed which all should trample. . . .

Yet such is the state of all moral virtue, that it is always uncertain and variable, sometimes extending to the whole compass of duty, and sometimes shrinking into a narrow space, and fortifying only a few avenues of the heart, while all the rest is left open to the incursions of appetite, or given up to the dominion of wickedness. Nothing therefore is more unjust than to judge of man by too short an acquaintance, and too slight inspection; for it often happens, that in the loose, and thoughtless, and dissipated, there is a secret radical worth, which may shoot out by proper cultivation; that the spark of heaven, though dimmed and obstructed, is yet not extinguished, but may by the breath of counsel and exhortation be kindled into flame.

To imagine that every one who is not completely good is irrecoverably abandoned, is to suppose that all are capable of the same degrees of excellence; it is indeed to exact from all that perfection which none ever can attain. And since the purest virtue is consistent with some vice, and the virtue of the greatest number with almost an equal proportion of contrary qualities, let none too hastily conclude that all goodness is lost, though it may for a time be clouded and overwhelmed; for most minds are the slaves of external circumstances, and conform to any hand that undertakes to mould them, roll down any torrent of custom in which they happen to be caught, or bend to any importunity that bears hard against them.

JOHNSON, *THE RAMBLER* (NO. 70), 115.

THE NECESSITY OF GOOD HUMOR

Those who exalt themselves into the chair of instruction, without enquiring whether any will submit to their authority, have not sufficiently considered how much of human life passes in little incidents, cursory conversation, slight business, and casual amusements; and therefore they have endeavoured only to inculcate the more awful virtues, without condescending to regard those petty qualities, which grow important only by their frequency, and which though they produce no single acts of heroism, nor astonish us by great events, yet are every moment exerting their influence upon us, and make the draught of life sweet or bitter by imperceptible instillations. They operate unseen and unregarded, as change of air makes us sick or healthy, though we breathe it without attention, and only know the particles that impregnate it by their salutary or malignant effects. . . .

Without good humour, learning and bravery can only confer that superiority which swells the heart of the lion in the desert, where he roars without reply, and ravages without resistance. Without good humour, virtue may awe by its dignity, and amaze by its brightness; but must always be viewed at a distance, and will scarcely gain a friend or attract an imitator.

Good humour may be defined as a habit of being pleased; a constant and perennial softness of manner, easiness of approach, and suavity of disposition; like that which every man perceives in himself, when the first transports of new felicity have subsided, and his thoughts are only kept in motion by a slow succession of soft impulses. Good humour is a state between gayety and unconcern; the act or emanation of a mind at leisure to regard the gratification of another.

JOHNSON, *THE RAMBLER* (NO. 72), 117.

RIGHT AND WRONG, FREEDOM AND RESPONSIBILITY

We can distinguish right from wrong—we feel the attraction to right and the repulsion from wrong, and so come to acknowledge our responsibility. . . . If a boy has been behaving rudely in a room, and you take him by the back of the neck and put him the other side of the door, there is no moral action on the part of the boy. But if you go to him and say, "Now you have not been behaving well—the right thing for you to do is to *go* till you can behave better," then he is free to choose whether he will go or not. We feel attracted to the right, but we are not compelled to do it. What, then, does it come to? . . . A sense of duty. I ought. That is a great point to have reached! I know the difference between right and wrong, I feel the responsibility, I know I am free, but I feel I ought—it is my duty. That is a magnificent standpoint—when we come to acknowledge that it is our duty to do right, not in the abstract, but for me. And I think this is thoroughly a part of human nature. How often we hear people say, "How vexed I am with myself!" Why do you feel vexed? Because you have done something you feel you ought not to have done or left something undone that you ought to have done. Such words as *vexation* and *remorse,* and *unworthy* and *base,* and on the other hand *amiable* and *good* show that we can distinguish between right and wrong.

KING, DUTY AND CONSCIENCE, 21–22.

THE ENMITY BETWEEN RIGHT AND WRONG

That Right and Wrong are in some sense the great adversaries, that they have been so since the foundation of the world, most persons practically acknowledge, even those who in theory contend that right and wrong can be resolved into the expedient and the inexpedient, or that one is only a modification of the other. What the Scripture adds to this old and general belief is the assertion that Right is the nature of God; that a living Being, the Author of this Universe and all which is in it, is pledged to assert and vindicate the Right; that Wrong is a lie and a rebellion; and that, yielding to it, we yield to the father of lies, to him who would not abide in the truth. Starting from that primary maxim, it goes on to affirm that Christ, the Son of God, took on Him the nature of man, that He might wrestle with this enemy of Right and Truth, and might deliver man from him. And thence it proceeds to that which is essentially and characteristically the New Testament doctrine, that which St. Paul is everywhere asserting, that the Spirit of the Father and the Son is wrestling in the great human society, is wrestling in each nation and in each man, with that spirit of Wrong and Untruth.

MAURICE, LESSONS OF HOPE, 135–36.

THE RIGHT SELF-LOVE

It is the fashion at the present moment to disparage the religious anxiety to save our own souls. The hope of heaven and the fear of hell are by our modern prophets widely decried or disparaged as selfish and unworthy motives. But this is really neither scriptural nor sensible, because after all there is a right kind of self-love. I never like the modern substitution of "selflessness" for unselfishness. For the self is a divine reality, and we are bound to preserve it. The golden rule is "thou shalt love thy neighbour"— not instead of thyself but—"as thyself." In fact the instinct of self-preservation is not a sin or a defect, but a fundamental and God-given instinct, inherent in everything that has life, and most of all in that which has the highest kind of life—in the soul or self of man. And if it be possible, as our Lord so solemnly and repeatedly warns us that it is—if it be possible by wilfulness, carelessness and sin fundamentally to ruin our very selves, our very fundamental being, and if hell means the state of those who have thus finally and fundamentally ruined themselves, there must come over any one who chooses to think a shivering horror at the awful possibility which lies before him—a horror which must, by the very constitution of human nature, become a motive for avoiding with all deliberate care the kinds of action which lead to self-ruin. Moreover, all experience shows us that it is only this care for our own souls which can enable us to fulfil our function in society. How many public careers, which might in greater or smaller degree have been careers of public usefulness, have been destroyed by private sins! How many undertakings, which might serve a useful purpose, are baffled and sometimes rendered impossible by the private jealousies, obstinacies, uncharitablenesses, ambitions of this or that individual! S. Paul was quite right, when he was exalting the glorious privilege of being a fellow worker with God, to go on at once to speak of being studious to avoid private sins, of giving diligence that his ministry be not blamed, lest his service of God be thwarted by obstacles interposed by his own defects. From every point of view we need the most diligent care of our own souls, for truly our own soul is a trust. . . .

It is very hard to be a good Christian. We inherit, so the Christian doctrine tells us, a fallen nature. I will not enlarge upon that, save by saying that all experience seems to verify the doctrine. It is not only progress we need but redemption; and our redemption was purchased for us at a tremendous price. Not with corruptible things such as silver and gold were we redeemed, but by something of inconceivable value, even by the precious blood of Him who sacrificed Himself that we might live. How can we then take our salvation lightly? Surely we must, as S. Peter says, "pass the time of our sojourning here in fear" [1 Pet 1:17]. . . . The fact is, so many men live habitually without the sense of God, and are then full of complaints that the Christian standard is impossibly high. It is high but possible; but it is possible only if we will steadily face the fact that we can live to the true only by deliberately dying to the false.

Christ died to sin, S. Paul says. He deliberately refused it and turned His back upon it. That is why the world of sin put Him to death. His death upon the Cross was a death to sin. But thus dying to sin He lives to God. And that law of living through dying—living in the true life by dying to the false—is the law for Christians, as it was the law of Christ's own life. The only way to live the life that is life indeed is to die to the life which disfigures, dishonours, and corrupts our manhood.

GORE, CHRISTIAN MORAL PRINCIPLES, 98–101.

THE RESOLUTE TRAVELER

Irresolution and mutability are often the faults of men whose views are wide and whose imagination is vigorous and excursive because they cannot confine their thoughts within their own boundaries of action, but are continually ranging over all the scenes of human existence, and consequently, are often apt to conceive that they fall upon new regions of pleasure, and start new possibilities of happiness. Thus they are busied with a perpetual succession of schemes, and pass their lives in alternate elation and sorrow, for want of that calm and immoveable acquiescence in their condition, by which men of slower understandings are fixed for ever to a certain point, or led on in the plain beaten track, which their fathers, and grandsires, have trod before them. . . .

Thus men may be made inconstant by virtue and by vice, by too much or too little thought; yet inconstancy, however dignified by its motives, is always to be avoided, because life allows us but a small time for enquiry and experiment, and he that steadily endeavours at excellence, in whatever employment, will more benefit mankind than he that hesitates in choosing his part till he is called to the performance. The traveller that resolutely follows a rough and winding path will sooner reach the end of his journey than he that is always changing his direction and wastes the hours of daylight in looking for smoother ground and shorter passages.

JOHNSON, THE RAMBLER (NO. 63), 106.

PRIDE AND PIETY

No people have more occasion to be afraid of the approaches of pride than those who have made some advances in a pious life. For pride can grow as well upon our virtues as upon our vices, and steals upon us on all occasions.

Every good thought that we have, every good action that we do, lays us open to pride and exposes us to the assaults of vanity and self-satisfaction.

LAW, *A SERIOUS CALL*, 214.

REASON AND PRIDE

God Almighty has entrusted us with the use of reason, and we use it to the disorder and corruption of our nature. We reason ourselves into all kinds of folly and misery, and make our lives the sport of foolish and extravagant passions, seeking after imaginary happiness in all kinds of shapes, creating to ourselves a thousand wants, amusing our hearts with false hopes and fears, using the world worse than irrational animals, envying, vexing, and tormenting one another with restless passions and unreasonable contentions.

Let any man but look back upon his own life and see what use he has made of his reason, how little he has consulted it, and how less he has followed it. What foolish passions, what vain thoughts, what needless labors, what extravagant projects, have taken up the greatest part of his life. How foolish he has been in his words and conversation, how seldom he has done well with judgment, and how often he has been kept from doing ill by accident: how seldom he has been able to please himself, and how often he has displeased others; how often he has changed his counsels, hated what he loved and loved what he hated; how often he has been enraged and transported at trifles, pleased and displeased with the very same things, and constantly changing from one vanity to another. Let a man but take this view of his own life, and he will see reason enough to confess that pride was not made for man.

LAW, *A SERIOUS CALL*, 215–16.

SELF-REGARD

Screwtape to Wormwood:

[T]housands of humans have been brought to think that humility means pretty women trying to believe they are ugly and clever men trying to believe they are fools. And since what they are trying to believe may, in some cases, be manifest nonsense, they cannot succeed in believing it, and we have the chance of keeping their minds endlessly revolving on themselves in an effort to achieve the impossible. To anticipate the Enemy's strategy, we must consider His aims. The Enemy [God] wants to bring the man to a state of mind in which he could design the best cathedral in the world, and know it to be the best, and rejoice in the fact, without being any more (or less) or otherwise glad at having done it than he would be if it had been done by another. The Enemy wants him, in the end, to be so free from any bias in his own favour that he can rejoice in his own talents as frankly and gratefully as in his neighbour's talents—or in a sunrise, an elephant, or a waterfall. He wants each man, in the long run, to be able to recognise all creatures (even himself) as glorious and excellent things. He wants to kill their animal self-love as soon as possible; but it is His long-term policy, I fear, to restore to them a new kind of self-love—a charity and gratitude for all selves, including their own: when they have really learned to love their neighbours as themselves, they will be allowed to love themselves as their neighbours.

LEWIS, THE SCREWTAPE LETTERS, 64–65.

9

Money

WASTING MONEY

If we waste our money, we are not only guilty of wasting a talent which God has given us, we are not only guilty of making that useless which is so powerful a means of doing good, but we do ourselves this further harm, that we turn this useful talent into a powerful means of corrupting ourselves; because so far as it is spent wrong so far it is spent in the support of some wrong temper, in gratifying some vain and unreasonable desires, in conforming to those fashions and pride of the world, which as Christians and reasonable men we are obliged to renounce. . . .

For so much as is spent in the vanity of dress may be reckoned so much laid out to fix vanity in our minds. So much as is laid out for idleness and indulgence may be reckoned so much given to render our hearts dull and sensual. . . .

So that on all accounts, whether we consider our fortune as a talent and trust from God, or the great good that it enables us to do, or the great harm that it does to ourselves if idly spent, on all these great accounts it appears that it is absolutely necessary to make reason and religion the strict rule of using all our fortune.

LAW, *A SERIOUS CALL*, 77–79.

A WAY TO MAKE AMENDS

What a large stock would the poor have to the fore, if Christians would but lay by for them all that they lay out in unnecessaries: nay, if they were but to have all that Christians lay out in sin and vanity, in pride, intemperance, etc., to comply with evil customs, etc.! And, in good truth, I cannot see how any Christian can make amends, such as will be accepted of God, for all his idle expenses: but by giving to the poor in some way proportionable to the money he has misspent, and what he has by him.

WILSON, *MAXIMS*, 13.

GIVE

Give, looking for nothing again, that is, without consideration of future advantages: give to children, to old men, to the unthankful, and the dying, and to those you shall never see again: for else your alms or curtesy is not charity, but traffick and merchandise: and be sure that you omit not to relieve the needs of your enemy and the injurious: for so possibly you may win him to your self; but do you intend the winning him to God.

TAYLOR, *HOLY LIVING*, 216–17.

MONEY IS OPPORTUNITY

It is good to give riches away—not because money is a bad thing: charity isn't like the hot penny in the children's game, which you pass on as fast as you can from hand to hand, since you are to lose a forfeit if you are caught holding it. No, the reason against holding much money is that money is power, money is opportunity, and your poor neighbours haven't got enough of it. Money is a serious subject. There is nothing more bogus than that affectation of aristocratic high-mindedness which considers the weighing of expenses to be beneath notice, and the paying of tailors' bills to be a bourgeois scruple.

FARRER, *THE END OF MAN*, 82.

THE RICH MAN

[The rich man] will not . . . look at the lives of Christians, to learn how he ought to spend his estate, but he will look into the scriptures and make every doctrine, parable, precept, or instruction that relates to rich men a law to himself in the use of his estate.

LAW, *A SERIOUS CALL*, 38.

THE PROBLEM OF MONEY

And so the problem of money gets all bound up with the problem of love, and cannot be separated from it. So far as the cry for more money, for better wages, which goes up from the underworld is a cry for more Life, more Beauty—more Truth—it is a cry which ought to find response in every man's heart, no matter what class or party he may belong to. It is not a party or a class cry—it is the cry of humanity for life, and the love of life and the fullness of life cannot be wrong, either in me or in the people of mean streets. Nevertheless, though love of money is mixed up with love of life, and the love of life is right, yet the love of money is all wrong, because it blinds our eyes to the meaning of life. It not only hardens our hearts, it softens our heads, when we think of life in terms of money, and not of money in terms of life.

STUDDERT KENNEDY, *THE WICKET GATE*, 157.

THE USE OF MONEY

But certainly our Lord had a suspicion of wealth; He had a suspicion of whatever allowed people to feel themselves a privileged class, or conduced to their regarding themselves as exceptional people who counted in God's sight for more than their fellows. So he had a suspicion of the learned class; but it expressed itself more often concerning the rich class. They would be the people who would instinctively feel that they were a privileged class, and that other people were to work for them; and it is upon that kind of feeling that He pours His tremendous irony. There are no two utterances of our Lord more tremendous than the parable of the Rich Fool and the parable of the Rich Man and Lazarus. There is nothing nearer to contempt to be found in our Lord's words. . . . So it was that our Lord welcomed continually manifest and open surrenders of wealth. That is what He suggested to the rich young man, who went away saddened thereby and reluctant. He proposed to him that he should give up all that he had and follow Him; and, short of that, you remember how the rich man Zaccheus, who held the obnoxious position of publican or farmer of the Roman taxes, when he was converted and subdued by his nearness to our Lord, stood out and made public profession of what he was going to do in the future. "Behold, Lord, from henceforth I give half of all I make to the poor; and if I can find in the past any wrong that I have done to any man, I hereby declare my intention to restore it fourfold" [Luke 19:8]. And this hearty act of renunciation Jesus met with His emphatic benediction. He loved these acts of renunciation, and He required the like act of renunciation from those who were to be His apostles. So when you move forward out of the Gospels into the Acts still you find these constant acts of renunciation. It is the habitual atmosphere. So great is the spirit of brotherhood that they had all things in common. There was no legislation to that effect; it was entirely voluntary. But these acts by which people sold their property and brought the produce and laid it at the apostles' feet for general distribution were common. . . .

If you go forward again out of New Testament times into the times that followed, and study the atmosphere of the early Christian Fathers . . . you will find a tremendous claim laid on wealth. There is a recognition of the law of private property as a necessary condition in the world—necessary in its fallen condition, necessary in a world of sin. But this law of private property is to be overshadowed by the law and principle of justice; and the law and principle of justice is that every man has a duty and right to work and to receive support adequate to his need. . . . And the people who have more than they need, and hold it back from those who have less than they need . . . are not merely uncharitable, but they fail to follow the law of justice, and the Fathers do not scruple to say that they steal what they selfishly withhold. That is the spirit of the Fathers.

GORE, *CHRISTIAN MORAL PRINCIPLES*, 84–88.

10

Wilderness Days

VICARIOUS SUFFERING

It is not hardships that are the wearing work of life. It is anxiety of heart and mind. . . . One sorrow, one deep, corroding anxiety, will wear deeper furrows in a cheek and brow than ten campaigns can do. One day's suspense will exhaust more, and leave the cheek paler, than a week's fasting.

. . . There is an anxiety about loss, about the consequences of misdoing, about a ruined reputation, about a narrowed sphere of action. . . . Observe . . . that sorrow, merely as sorrow, has in it no magical efficacy. . . . It is a great error when men, perceiving that God's natural penalties and hardships strengthen and purify the spirit, think to attain to a similar good by forcing such penalties and hardships upon themselves.

This is the blessedness of the suffering of Christ; it is the law of the Cross; it is the vicarious principle pervading life, that, voluntarily or involuntarily, we must suffer for others. If others are benefited involuntarily by our sufferings, then we do no more than the beasts who fulfill the law of their being unconsciously; who yield up their lives unwillingly, and therefore are not blessed by it. But if we are willing to bear our woe because we know that good will accrue, we know not how, or why, or when, to others, then we have indeed become partakers of Christ's Spirit, and learned a godlike lesson. To be willing to bear in order to teach others!—to lose, in order that others may "through us noblier live"—that is to know something of the blessedness He knew.

ROBERTSON, *LIVING THOUGHTS*, 202–3.

FORGET MISTAKES

We can all look back to past life and see mistakes that have been made, —to a certain extent, perhaps, irreparable ones. We can see where our education was fatally misdirected. The profession chosen for you perhaps was not the fittest, or you are out of place, and many things might have been better ordered. Now . . . it is wise to forget all that. It is not by regretting what is irreparable that true work is to be done, but by making the best of what we are. It is not by complaining that we have not the right tools, but by using well the tools we have. What we are, and where we are, is God's providential arrangement—God's doing, though it may be man's misdoing; and the manly and the wise way is to look your disadvantages in the face, and see what can be made out of them. Life, like war, is a series of mistakes, and he is not the best Christian nor the best general who makes the fewest false steps. Poor mediocrity may secure that; but he is the best who wins the most splendid victories by the retrieval of mistakes. Forget mistakes: organize victory out of mistakes.

ROBERTSON, *LIVING THOUGHTS*, 105–6.

DESPAIR

Who ever comes into a Church to [declare] an *excommunication* against himselfe? And shall any sad soule come hither, to gather arguments, from our preaching, to *excommunicate* it selfe, or to pronounce an impossibility upon her owne salvation? *God did a new thing*, says *Moses*, a strange thing, a thing never done before, when the earth opened her mouth and *Dathan*, and *Abiram* went downe quicke into the pit. Wilt thou doe a stranger thing then that? To teare open the jawes of Earth, and Hell, and cast thy self actually and really into it, out of a mis-imagination, that God hath cast thee into it before? Wilt thou force God to second thy irreligious *melancholy*, and to condemne thee at last, because thou hadst precondemned thy selfe, and renounced his mercy?

DONNE, *DONNE'S SERMONS*, 133.

STRENGTH AND STRUGGLE

You may go on through the crowded streets of heaven, asking each saint how he came there, and you will look in vain everywhere for a man morally and spiritually strong, whose strength did not come to him in struggle. Will you take the man who never had a disappointment, who never knew a want, whose friends all love him, whose health never knew a suspicion of its perfectness, on whom every sun shines, and against whose sails all winds, as if by special commission, are sent to blow, who still is great and good and true and unselfish and holy, as happy in his inner as in his outer life? Was there no struggle there? Do you suppose that man has never wrestled with his own success and happiness, that he has never prayed and emphasized his prayer with labor, "In all time of my prosperity, Good Lord, deliver me!" "Deliver me!" That is the cry of a man in danger, of a man with an antagonist. For years that man and his prosperity have been looking each other in the face and grappling one another—and that is a supremacy that was not won without a struggle, than which there is no harder on the earth.

BROOKS, IN ALLEN, *LIFE AND LETTERS*, 361.

ANXIETY ABOUT THE FUTURE

Evil is uncertain in the same degree as good, and for the reason that we ought not to hope too securely, we ought not to fear with too much dejection. The state of the world is continually changing, and none can tell the result of the next vicissitude. Whatever is afloat in the stream of time, may, when it is very near us, be driven away by an accidental blast, which shall happen to cross the general course of the current. . . . Our enemies may become weak, or we grow strong before our encounter, or we may advance against each other without ever meeting. There are, indeed, natural evils which we can flatter ourselves with no hopes of escaping, and with little of delaying; but of the ills which are apprehended from human malignity, or the opposition of rival interests, we may always alleviate the terror by considering that our persecutors are weak and ignorant, and mortal like ourselves. The misfortunes which arise from the concurrence of unhappy incidents should never be suffered to disturb us before they happen; because, if the breast be once laid open to the dread of mere possibilities of misery, life must be given a prey to dismal solicitude, and quiet must be lost for ever.

It is remarked by old Cornaro, that it is absurd to be afraid of the natural dissolution of the body, because it must certainly happen, and can, by no caution or artifice, be avoided. Whether this sentiment be entirely just, I shall not examine; but certainly, if it be improper to fear events which must happen, it is yet more evidently contrary to right reason to fear those which may never happen, and which, if they should come upon us, we cannot resist.

As we ought not to give way to fear, any more than indulgence to hope, because the objects both of fear and hope are yet uncertain, so we ought not to trust the representations of one more than of the other, because they are both equally fallacious; as hope enlarges happiness, fear aggravates calamity. It is generally allowed, that no man ever found the happiness of possession proportionate to that expectation which incited his desire, and invigorated his pursuit; nor has any man found the evils of life so formidable in reality, as they were described to him by his own imagination; every species of distress brings with it some peculiar supports, some unforeseen means of resisting, or power of enduring. . . . It is . . . sufficient that you are able to encounter the temptations which now assault you; when God sends trials, he may send strength.

All fear is in itself painful, and when it conduces not to safety is painful without use. Every consideration, therefore, by which groundless terrors may be removed, adds something to human happiness. It is likewise not unworthy of remark, that in proportion as our cares are employed upon the future, they are abstracted from the present, from the only time which we can call our own. . . .

JOHNSON, *THE RAMBLER* (NO. 29), 57.

THE ANTIDOTE

The safe and general antidote against sorrow is employment. . . .

Sorrow is a kind of rust of the soul, which every new idea contributes in its passage to scour away. It is the putrefaction of stagnant life, and is remedied by exercise and motion.

JOHNSON, *THE RAMBLER* (NO. 47), 84.

THE BURDEN OF LIFE

Your load of care, whatever it be that takes away the light heart, and makes the weeks seem slow, and oppresses you with a sense of dissatisfaction with what you have, and envy for others who seem so much brighter: this you may cast into the strong flood of a busy stir in life. In ceaseless occupation some have tried to get rid of their burden of troubled thoughts. There are men who dare not be alone an hour, or idle a day: they have that within which they must forget, and it can only be forgotten by keeping busy. This, however, is but an exchange of burdens; it is like shifting the burden from one shoulder to another; it is curing unrest by a new and fresh unrest. Or if, for a while the old burden disappear, if the torrent sweep it away out of sight, yet shall it he like bread cast upon the waters, to return again after many days. And the time comes when no man can work; the latter hours when the world with its activities, retiring, leaves the man alone; and the flood of the years which bore the load away will sweep about again and cast it, an unwelcome object, at his feet, who thenceforth can be rid of it no more. In a very busy life the pain of a heart that knoweth its own bitterness may for some time be stilled but the evening of such a life will not be light and pleasant, but full of clouds denser far than those of the heavy day.

DIX, CHRIST AT THE DOOR, 198–99.

THE NEARNESS OF GOD

Dear brethren: half the sorrow of our lives would be turned to joy, and the rest would be assuaged, did we but believe and act on the belief that our God is an ever present help in trouble. It is the beginning and the end, the substance and the sum of our religion in its personal application, that God is near to every one of us. . . . Every man has his burden to bear; every heart knoweth its own bitterness. But what we know, God also knows; and of all that wend their way through this troubled world, not one but is seen of the Father; and of all the hearts that ever ached, or shall hereafter ache, not one aches uncared-for: nor is any sufferer overlooked, nor does any one drink, unnoticed, the cup of bitterness. There are no terms strong enough to state our conviction, that, as a literal fact, the Lord knows and numbers the very hairs of our heads; that He is most intimately acquainted with every human sorrow; that He sees every tear that falls, and hears even the lowest moan of distress; that He weighs, counts, and measures, and recollects; that when we are in our trial, He observes how we take it; that when we are under pressure He marks how we endure; that He is near us from the beginning to the end; with little children, understanding their child-sorrows, even when by their own parents they are misunderstood; with the young in their buoyant days, and later when disenchantment comes and ideals fade away; with the ripe in years, who measure their strength against the great storms of maturity; and with us in the latter time, when the prospect saddens, and the shadows of the evening are stretched out. There are those to whom this faith of ours is foolishness; but observe what they say, and you will find that they have never given you anything in its place; they never will: they cannot, for there is nothing else to give. Thou hast thy burden, of necessity or want, of hard work and dull hours bringing little or no good, of anxiety about others or fears for thyself; of buried hope or affections wasted on unworthy objects; of spiritual dryness, or lack of earnest faith; of longing for the unattainable or regret for the irreparable: whatever it be, bring that sorrow straight to thy God, with the conviction that it is the only rational and sensible thing to do, that all other expedients are vain, that there is no help in the world, or in any child of man, or anywhere out of Him; and surely the crooked shall be made straight and the rough places plain, and thou shalt find in the Lord a comfort not to be had apart from him. . . .

DIX, *CHRIST AT THE DOOR*, 203–5.

NOT ABOVE THE MASTER

If Christ had to be made perfect by sufferings, much more must we. If he needed to learn obedience by sorrow, much more must we. If he needed in the days of his flesh, to make supplication to God his Father with strong crying and tears, so do we. And if he was heard in that he feared, so, I trust, we shall be heard likewise. If he needed to taste even the most horrible misery of all; to feel for a moment that God had forsaken him; surely we must expect, if we are to be made like him, to have to drink at least one drop out of his bitter cup. It is very wonderful: but yet it is full of hope and comfort. Full of hope and comfort to be able, in our darkest and bitterest sorrow, to look up to heaven and say, At least there is one who has been through all this. As Christ was, so are we in this world; and the disciple cannot be above his master. Yes, we are in this world as he was, and he was once in this world as we are. He has been through all this, and more. He knows all this and more. "We have a High Priest above us who can be touched with the feeling of our infirmities, because he has been tempted in all things like as we are, yet without sin" [Heb 4:15].

KINGSLEY, *THE GOOD NEWS OF GOD*, 261–62.

ON EAGLES' WINGS

We all know by a hundred wretched experiences the impotence of an unnerved will, the poverty of a corrupt love. Our resolutions are so brave until the moment comes for keeping them; our intentions are so excellent until the pressure of facts confuses us; our desires are so eager for purity, if only they would not so strangely languish just as the passions awake in a storm. All would be well if we did not just slip and fall where it was vital to stand. Most miserable this incessant collapse! How it disheartens; how it disgusts! We are netted as a bird. We flutter up, but the meshes once again entangle us, and down we come to the ground, and the sky is as far off as ever. And what if, around and about this poor, this impoverished will, there was wrapped the irresistible might of a will that had not been broken, a will, new, fresh, undaunted, tough as steel, endurable as stone, firm as adamant?—what if the warmth of a love were laid about it to which the emotions of impure appetites are impossible?—what if we were given up to this love, so that it abode within us and possessed us, and held us fast, untroubled by our disasters, unhurt by our sins?—what if, after all our sinning, we still could turn back again and again to find this loving will there still, pure and strong as ever within us, still pressing, with unwearied patience, on towards the beauty of holiness, with its unwavering eyes ever fixed on the Face of God? Would not this be enough? would not this be salvation? would not this be peace ? "Ye shall mount on eagles' wings." That is our splendid assurance. No longer that fluttering tumult of the poor captives, tangled in the snare! Nay! but "on eagles' wings"—the wings of God under us, kingly and unconquerable, as they beat their strong way upwards, let the winds blow as they may "on eagles' wings"—the wings of a holy will, the wings of a clean desire laid under us to bear us upwards. This may be yours, you who are in sickness, infirm, or palsied, or dead. This uplifting power may be made your own, if you will but forsake your own mode of cure, your own medicines, your own wisdom, and come and lay yourself at the feet of Him Who alone can make a breach in your sad captivity. Who, through His very Manhood has, alone, the power here on earth to forgive the sins of His fellows.

HOLLAND, *HELPS*, 99–101.

THE TRIUMPH OF LOVE

We celebrate the Resurrection-triumph of Incarnate love. We long to share that triumph. But that can only be so if triumphant love is in our souls. And the triumph of love must be over the enemies of love, which are hatred and malice, envy and contempt, suspicion and indifference.

The Easter message proclaims the triumph of Love over all of these. But it wins by suffering. If we show love in the face of hatred, we must not expect to overcome the hatred without suffering. It is by its suffering that love prevails; that is the message of Good Friday. But through its suffering it does prevail; that is the message of Easter Day. The Resurrection proclaims that the only real success is that which is in store for those who love, and will practice a chivalry, even a knight-errantry, which to the world must seem grotesque. We are to trust the untrustworthy and love the unlovely, accepting the misery of betrayals and ingratitude, until our constancy in loving and trusting softens and wins the malignant or the suspicious heart. We are to heap up the coals of fire on the head of the unloving, as the blacksmith heaps the glowing coals on the iron bar, till hardness gives place to malleability and we overcome evil with good.

The man who lives thus in our fallen world will suffer; say, rather, the Man who did once live thus in our fallen world did suffer. But if we hold fast to Him He carries us to the triumph that He Himself has won, the triumph of love over hatred and malice, over envy and contempt, over suspicion and indifference—even over Death, which is Love's last enemy because it seems to rob Love of its beloved. To such a triumph we look forward. It cannot be completed under the conditions of life upon this planet. But even here it can be tasted. We look forward to a world where mutual trust is universal, where each success or failure wins from all a genuine sympathy in joy or sorrow, where every man and woman, where every society and nation, where every house of business or manufacturing firm, where every branch of the Christian Church, sincerely desires and rejoices at the well-being of every other. But that can only come if those who believe in such an order will live even now as members of it, suffering in this world whatever their loyalty to that heavenly citizenship involves. For it is not in spite of its anguish in this world, but in and through that anguish, that Love wins the victory.

TEMPLE, *FELLOWSHIP WITH GOD*, 182–84.

ACQUAINTANCE WITH MISERY

An overmastering sense of human ills can be taken as the world's invitation to deny her Maker, or it may be taken as God's invitation to succor his world. Which is it to be? Those who take the practical alternative become more closely and more widely acquainted with misery than the onlookers; but they feel the grain of existence, and the movement of the purposes of God. They do not argue, they love; and what is loved is always known as good. The more we love, the more we feel the evils besetting or corrupting the object of our love. But the more we feel the force of the besetting harms, the more certain we are of the value residing in what they attack; and in resisting them are identified with the action of God, whose mercy is over all flesh.

FARRER, *LOVE ALMIGHTY*, 164–65.

11

Patience, Pardon, and Perseverance

REPENTANCE

When Jesus urged men to repent, He was urging them to become as little children. He wasn't asking them to eat the dust. He was confronting them with the necessity of a radical change of outlook, a fundamental re-orientation of their lives, so that they would no longer trust for security in the persona they had built up—the drama of being me which I continuously stage for my own benefit—so that they would no longer trust that, but have the courage to become as receptive as little children, with all the openness to life, the taking down of the shutters and the throwing away of the armour which that entails. . . .

It's obvious how important repentance is for the Christian. It was part of the basic message of Jesus. He began his ministry by telling men to repent and believe in the gospel. Unless, therefore, we are willing to repent, we cannot be His disciples. . . .

[This] is what repentance means: discovering that you have more to you than you dreamt or knew, becoming bored with being only a quarter of what you are and therefore taking the risk of surrendering to the whole, and thus finding more abundant life. . . .

WILLIAMS, *THE TRUE WILDERNESS*, 76, 80, 82.

BREAKING AND RE-MAKING

"I can never forgive myself. I've done it and there's no going back on it. But I made a colossal mistake. I've damaged the people I love. I can never forgive myself."

Haven't you heard some such confession as that? Haven't you made such a confession?

How bitter it is! A cutting word spoken which can never be re-called, or a rotten deed done which can never be undone. "I'll never forgive myself." He thought he was such a fine type, and to think he could sink to that! The bubble of his pride has been pricked. He has been humiliated by his own act. He is utterly disillusioned—not with others but—with himself. He has let himself down. The rest of life is lived under an enormous burden of guilt.

Here indeed is a crisis! If nothing can be done about it, he will go through life warped and twisted and embittered. There is only One that can handle that crisis effectively, and that is Christ.

Let me tell you what I mean.

This crisis of disillusionment with self can be a disaster. But it can equally be the beginning of new life. For look at what has happened. Someone has seen that he is not quite so good a fellow as he previously imagined. On the contrary, there is a weakness, a core of rottenness, which has led to disaster.

We are sinners, we need God's forgiveness and re-instatement. We need to be made new creatures. But is that possible?

The answer is in a true story.

Simon Peter had reason to believe he was a bit of a lad. At least so he thought.

Was he not the leader of the band of apostles? Had not he had that wonderful flash of inspiration which enabled him to confess Jesus as the Christ of God? Had he not sworn that, though all others might forsake Jesus and flee, he never would? Didn't he mean every word of that? Of course he did. Then that wretched servant girl who curled her lip at him and laughed at him for being a follower of Jesus caused all the trouble. Talk about a pricked balloon! He had collapsed. He had denied his Lord, with cursings and swearings.

What a fool he had been! What a sinner to let his Lord down! "I'll never forgive myself," he muttered. "I'm utterly disillusioned with my-self. How can I forgive myself after what I've done?"

It was not long after that the risen Jesus met him and took him on one side. "Now it's coming," Peter must have thought. "He'll dismiss me, and that will be the end. After all, that's all I can expect."

The reverse happened. "Do you love me, Peter?" "Of course I do, Lord."

"Then there's work for you to do. You are a forgiven man. Go—and feed my sheep.

Go—and tend my lambs."

If Jesus could forgive like that, how could Peter continue unforgiving to himself? There was no need for disillusionment any longer. He was now a man re-made, re-commissioned.

It is at that point that life begins.

The re-making began with the breaking.

When Jesus turned and looked on Peter, he went outside and wept.

"Lord Jesus, look on me."

COGGAN, *CONVICTIONS*, 203–4.

PATIENCE

I often think that the spiritual life is very much like gardening, and most of the worst mistakes we make in it, after we have seriously given ourselves to it, are just those mistakes an inexperienced gardener makes. The idea that a good vigorous campaign with a pitch fork is the best way of extirpating tiresome weeds from an herbacious border is the one we most have to unlearn. We plunge in, toss the ground violently in every direction, pluck out the weeds, make a big pile, and retire in a state of moist satisfaction saying we've done a very good morning's work.

But have we? We've disturbed the roots of the best perennials. We've knocked off some shoots. We've grubbed up loads of little modest seedlings springing up in odd corners. And in our hurry, we have broken weeds and left the bottom half of their stems in the ground to start a vigorous life again.

An expert doesn't do it like that. That kind of a gardener drops to the knees with a hand fork and works [carefully], bit by bit. . . . That patient, quiet work is the foundation of a good garden: gently keeping the ground in order, picking off slugs and snails, and tending the plants that will grow. Good gardening is not feverishly sticking in geraniums to get a transient show of bloom.

After all, it is God, not you, who settles what sort of garden [your soul] is to be. Your job is strictly confined to making it as good as it can be of its sort. You may want the predominate character to be contemplative and devotional. You would like your soul to grow fragile and beautiful flowers. But perhaps He doesn't want a contemplative just there. It may suit Him better to plant you in potatoes. That is less interesting of course, but just as essential to His plan.

Patience involves a cheerful acceptance of that and settles down to see that the potatoes are as good as you can get them to be. That, not the self-chosen growing of prize chrysanthemums, is the spirit of a good and faithful servant who will be able at the end to repeat the words of the Master: "I have finished the work You gave me to do, not the work I decided to do for You. I do not have the startling achievement my admiring followers expected. But I have worked hard in Your secret purposes which I have taken bit by bit from your hand. The work has been done in the wet and the cold and the fog, in weakness and exhaustion, steadily, patiently, and solely for you. And it has had a mysterious efficacy out of proportion to its apparent success."

The Cross, the death of self, enters deeply into such a career. I often think that it will not be the successful and impressive religious person, but the quiet, insignificant workers and sufferers, the obscure, the drudges, and the failures who will be able to say at the end with Christ, "It is finished! It is complete!"

It is those who, by simple faith and patient correspondence with God's requirements given bit by bit, whose quiet homely heroism is so easily ignored and yet so difficult, those who will be able to say: "I, in my tiny way, have glorified You on earth. I have finished the work You gave me to do."

UNDERHILL, THE WAYS OF THE SPIRIT, 172–73.

FORGIVENESS

In the case of God, grace often takes the form of forgiveness. There is an interesting story which Jesus once told in one of his parables. He told of a man to whom two other men were in debt. One owed a colossal sum; the other a comparatively paltry one. But they were both in the same boat— they were both stony-broke, both totally bankrupt. What was the man to do? He might, according to the custom of the day, clap them both into gaol. Or he might, I suppose, make them set about the process of trying to pay back what they owed—quite likely a sheer impossibility. He took neither course. "He graced them both," says the parable. "He forgave them both." They could do nothing but accept the man's graciousness with infinite gratitude, and go out to start a new life under, I imagine, a totally new relationship with the man who had "graced" them.

Forgiveness is a costly thing. You know that, if you have ever forgiven anyone who has deeply hurt you or wronged you. A costly forgiveness lies at the heart of the Christian Gospel. It is the love of God in action, going out to man in his need of forgiveness. Love doesn't constantly reckon up the long list of our sins and refuse to do anything about us till we improve. If that were the case, we should indeed be in a bad way. Here is one of the great differences between the Old Testament and the New. In the Old Testament we are told over and over that "the Lord loves the righteous." The New Testament gives us the joyous assurance that while we were yet sinners Christ died for us—such was the measure of his love! The picture of the Good Shepherd who is not content with the ninety-nine safely in the fold; who does not wait for the hundredth sheep to find its own way back; but, rather, leaves the ninety-nine in their security, breasts the dangers of wind and precipice and searches for the sheep until he finds it—this is the good news of the Gospel. What should I have had to say to the young alcoholic who came to see me recently, having made a mess of his life, and who said to me: "Will God really forgive me all the awful things I have done?"—what should I have said if I had not believed the utter truth of the forgiveness of sins, at the cost of Christ's death, and the basic truth of the grace of God, God's love in action going out to people like that alcoholic and to me? He and I—both of us—need more than a teacher, more than an example, more than a code of ethics. We need a Saviour who in infinite mercy goes out after us, even when we have run away from him. All he asks is that we turn round and face him, and throw ourselves into the arms of his mercy.

COGGAN, *THE HEART OF THE CHRISTIAN FAITH*, 43–44.

PATIENCE WITH OURSELVES

Next comes long-suffering and gentleness in dealing with our own souls and unsatisfactory lives. Only the Peace of God, a constant turning in our prayers to His abiding tranquility, is going to teach us that and make us realize that patience with ourselves is a duty for Christians and the only real humility. For it means patience with a growing creature whom God has taken in hand and whose completion He will effect in His own time and His own way.

UNDERHILL, *THE FRUITS OF THE SPIRIT*, 25.

PARDON FOR WHAT WE HAVE BEEN

Past guilt lies behind us, and is well forgotten. There is a way in which even sin may be banished from the memory. If a man looks forward to the evil he is going to commit, and satisfies himself that it is inevitable, and so treats it lightly, he is acting as a fatalist. But if a man partially does this, looking backward, feeling that sin when it is past has become part of the history of God's universe, and is not to be wept over for ever, he only does that which the Giver of the Gospel permits him to do. Bad as the results have been in the world of making light of sin, those of brooding over it too much have been worse. Remorse has done more harm than even hardihood. It was remorse which fixed Judas in an unalterable destiny . . . ; it is remorse which so remembers bygone faults as to paralyze the energies for doing Christ's work; for when you break a Christian's spirit, it is all over with progress. . . . You remember how Christ treated sin. Sin of oppression and hypocrisy indignantly, but sin of frailty—"'Hath no man condemned thee?' 'No man, Lord.' 'Neither do I condemn thee, go and sin no more'" [John 8:10–11]. As if He would bid us think more of what we may be than of what we have been.

ROBERTSON, *SERMONS*,79–80.

FORGIVING OTHERS

One of the most astonishing things that Jesus Christ ever said was that men cannot hope to be forgiven by God unless they are prepared to forgive the people who offend or hurt them. I sometimes think this searching truth has been soft-pedalled, but it's very evident in the Gospels. Every time we say the Lord's Prayer we say, "Forgive us our trespasses as we forgive them that trespass against us," and Jesus added: "For if you forgive other people their failures your Heavenly Father will also forgive you: but if you will not forgive other people neither will your Heavenly Father forgive your failures" [Matt 6:14–15].

If we could only see for a moment how much God is prepared to forgive us, and how comparatively little we are prepared to forgive other people, we might have a good laugh at ourselves, which would do us a lot of good, as well as help us to know much more of what being at peace with God means.

PHILLIPS, *THE NEWBORN CHRISTIAN*, 156.

FORGIVING OURSELVES

Like many others, I find myself something of a perfectionist. If we are not careful, this obsession for the perfect can make us arrogantly critical of other people, and, in certain moods, desperately critical of ourselves.

In this state of mind, it is not really that I cannot subscribe to the doctrine of the forgiveness of sins, but that the tyrannical super-Me condemns and has no mercy on myself.

John, in his wisdom, points out in these inspired words, that "if our hearts condemn us, *God is greater* than our heart, and knoweth all things" [1 John 3:20].

This is a gentle but salutary rebuke to our assumption that we know better than God!

PHILLIPS, *FOR THIS DAY*, 138.

TWO HINGES

As there is a death natural, and a death civil, so is there a death moral, both in philosophy and in divinity; and if a death, then consequently a resurrection too. Every great and notable change of our course of life, whereby we are not now any longer the same men that before we were, be it from worse to better, or from better to worse, is a moral death; a moral death to that we change from, and a moral resurrection to that we change to. If we change to the better, that is sin's death; if we alter to the worse, that is sin's resurrection. When we commit sin, we die, we are dead in sin; when we repent, we revive again; when we repent ourselves of our repenting and relapse back, then sin riseth again from the dead. . . . And even upon these two, as two hinges, turneth our whole life. All our life is spent in one of them.

ANDREWES, *NINETY-SIX SERMONS*, 202.

FAILURE

In our schooling, failure bears its part. It is no useless drag upon us. In failure lies our best lesson. It teaches, it trains, it shapes, it endows, quite as truly as our success. Nothing need be lost through failing, if only we be loyal to our lesson; if only we be brave under the buffets of experience.

Fruit is not here; but fruit may come hereafter—fruit in abundance, out of the very failure which pressed us down, and curtailed us, and sharply disciplined us here. Hereafter, it may be our failures that we shall bless most, as we see what they brought us. Who knows what is going on, in secret, behind these very failures in others, which most provoke us? The soul is being tamed, broken, humiliated; but it may be receiving, also, its glorification. Anyhow, it will not be the failure which distresses us, but only the failure to use the failure to good purposes. Our failures— above all, our noble failures—are part and parcel of our spiritual history, of our spiritual growth. When we go before our God, the failures will go to the great account; they will be elements in the judgment; they will be as instrumental and effective as any of our successes, in determining our eternal lot.

HOLLAND, *HELPS*, 9–10.

RE-CREATION OF THE PENITENT

Pardon, acceptance, peace, Heaven, are opened at once to all who, with penitent hearts, return to God through Jesus Christ our Lord. The love wherewith God receives returning prodigals hath its spring in His un-changing, unending love; the first gush of tears waters the seed which shall be reaped in everlasting joy. We are replaced, by repentance, on the road to life, whence we had wandered, yet at the beginning, not at the end; God does not take away trials, or carry us *over* them, but strengthens us *through* them. When He turns men to Himself; He changes their will, not their trials. Whereas before, forsaking His grace, they were defeated, *now,* through His grace, He gives them victory over their besetting sin. But there can be no victory without warfare, nor warfare without toil and pain. He turns men round that, whereas before they turned their backs on Him, henceforth they should hold Him before them, aim at Him, stretch towards Him, and He makes each act wherein they obey Him a step towards Himself and His everlasting love and bliss.

PUSEY, *SELECTIONS*, 307–8.

THE NECESSITY OF PATIENCE

So large a part of human life passes by in a state contrary to our natural desires, that one of the principal topics of moral instruction is the art of bearing calamities. And such is the certainty of evil, that it is the duty of every man to furnish his mind with those principles that may enable him to act under it with decency and propriety.

The sect of ancient philosophers, that boasted to have carried this necessary science to the highest perfection, were the Stoics, or scholars of Zeno, whose wild enthusiastic virtue pretended to an exemption from the sensibilities of unenlightened mortals, and who proclaimed themselves exalted, by the doctrines of their sect, above the reach of those miseries which embitter life to the rest of the world. They therefore removed pain, poverty, loss of friends, exile, and violent death, from the catalogue of evils; and passed, in their haughty stile, a kind of irreversible decree, by which they forbade them to be counted any longer among the objects of terror or anxiety, or to give any disturbance to the tranquility of a wise man.

This edict was, I think, not universally observed: for though one of the more resolute, when he was tortured by a violent disease, cried out, that let pain harrass him to its utmost power, it should never force him to consider it as other than indifferent and neutral; yet all had not stubbornness to hold out against their senses; for a weaker pupil of Zeno is recorded to have confessed in the anguish of the gout, that *he now found pain to be an evil.*

It may however be questioned, whether these philosophers can be very properly numbered among the teachers of patience; for if pain be not an evil, there seems no instruction requisite how it may be borne; and, therefore, when they endeavour to arm their followers with arguments against it, they may be thought to have given up their first position. But, such inconsistencies are to be expected from the greatest understandings, when they endeavour to grow eminent by singularity, and employ their strength in establishing opinions opposite to nature.

The controversy about the reality of external evils is now at an end. That life has many miseries, and that those miseries are, sometimes at least, equal to all the powers of fortitude, is now universally confessed; and therefore it is useful to consider not only how we may escape them, but by what means those which either the accidents of affairs, or the infirmities of nature must bring upon us, may be mitigated and lightened, and how we may make those hours less wretched, which the condition of our present existence will not allow to be very happy.

The cure for the greatest part of human miseries is not radical, but palliative. Infelicity is involved in corporeal nature, and interwoven with our being; all attempts therefore to decline it wholly are useless and vain: the armies of pain send their arrows against us on every side, the choice is only between those which are more or less sharp, or tinged with poison of greater or less malignity; and the strongest armour which reason can supply, will only blunt their points, but cannot repel them.

The great remedy which Heaven has put in our hands is patience, by which, though we cannot lessen the torments of the body, we can in a great measure preserve the peace of the mind, and shall suffer only the natural and genuine force of an evil, without heightening its acrimony, or prolonging its effects.

There is indeed nothing more unsuitable to the nature of man in any calamity than rage and turbulence, which, without examining whether they are not sometimes impious, are at least always offensive, and incline others rather to hate and despise than to pity and assist us. . . .

In those evils which are allotted to us by Providence, such as deformity, privation of any of the senses, or old age, it is always to be remembered, that impatience can have no present effect, but to deprive us of the consolations which our condition admits, by driving away from us those by whose conversation or advice we might be amused or helped. . . .

In all evils which admit a remedy, impatience is to be avoided, because it wastes that time and attention in complaints, that, if properly applied, might remove the cause. Turenne [seventeenth-century marshal of France, one of the greatest of French commanders], among the acknowledgments which he used to pay in conversation to the memory of those by whom he had been instructed in the art of war, mentioned one with honour, who taught him not to spend his time in regretting any mistake which he had made, but to set himself immediately and vigorously to repair it.

Patience and submission are very carefully to be distinguished from cowardice and indolence. We are not to repine, but we may lawfully struggle; for the calamities of life, like the necessities of nature, are calls to labour, and exercises of diligence. When we feel any pressure of distress, we are not to conclude that we can only obey the will of Heaven by languishing under it; any more than when we perceive the pain of thirst we are to imagine that water is prohibited. Of misfortune it never can be certainly known whether, as proceeding from the hand of God, it is an act of favour, or of punishment: but since all the ordinary dispensations of Providence are to be interpreted according to the general analogy of things, we may conclude, that we have a right to remove one inconvenience as well as another; that we are only to take care lest we purchase ease with guilt. . . .

The chief security against the fruitless anguish of impatience, must arise from frequent reflection on the wisdom and goodness of the God of nature, in whose hands are riches and poverty, honour and disgrace, pleasure and pain, and life and death. A settled conviction of the tendency of every thing to our good, and of the possibility of turning miseries into happiness, by receiving them rightly, will incline us to *bless the name of the Lord, whether he gives or takes away.*

JOHNSON, *THE RAMBLER* (NO. 32), 60–62.

PENITENCE AFTER A FALL

I find after some special failure through moral weakness or sin, there is special need of a special opportunity for great confidence in God. The mischief is done. One has given way, and one is tempted to despair for about a month, and cherish a thought in the background that one may come back to God in true penitence after some weeks of depression, as if that were necessary. But to give way to depression, we know, is to comfort the evil self which grace has to slay. The Evil One makes the most of our moral failure, if he can persuade us to be depressed and benumbed by it. Real humility and penitence do not ask, will not take, that "discontented retirement" from God under the trees in the shadow. Real humility will come straight out to God in the light at once, "Father, I have sinned," and takes the inward shadow as the punishment it has brought on itself, and bears it willingly for the glory of God, in the love of God; and God is glorified by our patience with our own worthlessness and by our confidence in Him. We must not wait for God to work a miracle on our character, to break our hard heart, but we must exercise humility and confidence, look up to Him, and give Him thanks for being what He is—the Eternal Love—none the less because of our unworthiness. We must anoint our own heart with the gifts of love, sorrow, confession, resolution—gifts of the Holy Spirit which we have in us by the grace of past sacraments.

When I have no comfort in myself, at my worst and darkest, I must believe in the Light, and kindle in my reason and will the Light which is in me, in spite of my depression in the sensitive soul.

My sin is not the reality, the thing to start from, to believe in; it is the unreal, the result of carelessness, and absence of love. Now, in my confession, love comes to life with my sorrow, and the opening of my grief; and though my heart seems hard and dead it is not so really; but my penitence begins in my conscience and reason, and is true there, though in the sensitive soul there is no feeling yet of the holy change of mind. One has to humble oneself quickly, and take more tenderly and gratefully than ever one's pardon, without waiting for feeling to come to life.

The matter lies between me, that is, my conscience and will, and God. Feeling is only accidentally associated with my repentance. I neither wait for it, nor trust it far; but only use it, if it is there, as a great help; or go to God with more . . . love that waits for no encouragement, if it is not there.

CONGREVE, SPIRITUAL LETTERS, 106–7.

FORGIVENESS OF SINS

The forgiveness of sins, in its fullest sense, signifies nothing less than the destruction of evil; and to believe in the forgiveness of sins implies the belief that evil can be destroyed, and that men can be set completely free from their bondage to it. Such a freedom is the glorious liberty of the Sons of God, into which, in the experience of Christians, Christ has the power to raise them. "This is a true saying, and worthy of all men to be received: that Christ Jesus came into the world to save sinners" [1 Tim 1:15].

STUDDERT KENNEDY, THE WICKET GATE, 176.

THE FORCE OF PERSEVERANCE

All the performances of human art, at which we look with praise or wonder, are instances of the resistless force of perseverance; it is by this that the quarry becomes a pyramid, and that distant countries are united with canals. If a man was to compare the effect of a single stroke of the pick-axe, or of one impression of the spade, with the general design and last result, he would be overwhelmed by the sense of their disproportion; yet those petty operations, incessantly continued, in time surmount the greatest difficulties, and mountains are levelled, and oceans bounded, by the slender force of human beings.

It is therefore of the utmost importance that those who have any intention of deviating from the beaten roads of life, and acquiring a reputation superior to names hourly swept away by time among the refuse of fame, should add to their reason, and their spirit, the power of persisting in their purposes; acquire the art of sapping what they cannot batter, and the habit of vanquishing obstinate resistance by obstinate attacks.

JOHNSON, THE RAMBLER (NO. 43), 77–78.

12

Marriage and Family

LOVE WHICH HATH ENDS WILL HAVE AN END

It is the worst clandestine marriage when God is not invited to it. Wherefore beforehand beg his gratious assistance. . . .

Deceive not thyself by overexpecting happinesse in the married estate. Look not therein for contentment greater than God will give, or a creature in this world can receive, namely to be free from all inconveniences. Marriage is not like the hill Olympus . . . wholly clear, without clouds; yea expect both wind and storms sometimes, which when blown over, the aire is the clearer, and wholsomer for it. . . .

Let Grace and Goodnesse be the principall loadstone of thy affections. For love which hath ends will have an end, whereas that founded in true virtue will alwayes continue. Some hold it unhappy to be married with a diamond ring, perchance . . . because the diamond hinders the roundnesse of the ring, ending the infinitenesse thereof, and seems to presage some termination in their love, which ought ever to endure. . . .

Neither chuse . . . for Beauty. A cried-up Beauty makes more for her own praise then her husbands profit. They tell us of a floting Iland in Scotland: but sure no wise pilot will cast anchor there, lest the land swimme away with his ship. So are they served (and justly enough) who onely fasten their love on fading Beauty, and both fail together.

FULLER, *THE HOLY STATE AND THE PROFANE STATE*, 212–13.

THE VOCATION OF MARRIAGE

[From Father Andrew's letter to a lady dated October 23, 1930:]

Men do not have to become Catholic to become children of God. If they are not even baptized it was their Father Who created them.

I shall pray for you often. You must, of course, make your own choice, but there are just three things I can say. (1) If you love this man and feel you would be glad for him to be the father of your children, that will make it right whatever happens. (2) Think of marriage as a vocation to a creative comradeship not with a saint but with that man, whoever he may be, whom God commends to you. (3) Live true to your own ideals and your own faith, but don't expect another to see with your eyes or to think with your thoughts; and be sure that religion is a life and not an argument.

LOVE AND LIFE

[From Father Andrew to the same lady, January 28, 1931:]

I saw your engagement definitely announced in *The Times*. I don't know who sent me the cutting. It just came in an envelope. . . .

I wish I was going to marry you two. Don't be afraid, my dear child. Welcome the adventure.

Love is the reason for life, and life is the opportunity of love. If love reigns in your heart and life, all will be well. Sometimes there is a coalition of suspicion, jealousy, and self-assertion, then all goes wrong, but if the one royalty of love is ruling, there will be peace in that state.

God bless and keep you always.

FATHER ANDREW, *LETTERS*, 194–95.

CHRISTIAN LOYALTY

The difference between a Catholic marriage and another lies in this: that [in a Christian marriage] each takes the other from God, and each makes the promises to God, and not in the presence of a man with a man's idea of faithfulness but in the presence of Christ Who was faithful to the unfaithful. In a registry office Jack promises Jill he will be true to her, and Jill Jack that she will be true to him, and that before the Registrar; in the Catholic Church Jack promises God he will be true to Jill and Jill promises God that she will be true to Jack, and that before the symbol of deathless loyalty, the Cross of Christ.

FATHER ANDREW, *LOVE'S FULFILLMENT*, 72.

MARRIAGE AND THE WIDER WORLD

In taking marriage into its sacramental structure, the Church breaks down the barrier between the sacred and the secular, declares its concern with our worldly, embodied existence, and provides for the impact of the divine grace upon our everyday activities. At first sight, it may seem strange that matrimony is reckoned a sacrament at all. Yet the recognition of its sacramental character forms an indispensable link between worship and life, and Christian marriage becomes the gateway through which the grace of holy Being made present in the sacraments can penetrate the wider world of human relationships. . . .

If prayer, worship, and the sacraments form the center of Christian life, then it must be said that the first concentric ring as one moves out from the center is the area of sex, marriage, and family life. The church has rightly seen that this area provides a bridgehead into the world, and that if these most intimate communal relations can be "sanctified," that is to say, made whole and healthy, then a decisive step has been taken toward eventually sanctifying the larger social relations that lie beyond.

Actually, it is not hard to see the immediate outreach of the sacramental idea beyond marriage and the family. The Christian doctrines of creation and incarnation, by recognizing the divine presence in the world and our own responsibility to cooperate with this presence in its work of creation-reconciliation-consummation, enable us to see the world and our policies of action in it with a new clarity and seriousness. The other person is seen as the neighbor, destined to have his place in the family of God. Even material things are to be seen in the light of Being and of our own status as stewards or shepherds or guardians of Being.

MACQUARRIE, *PRINCIPLES*, 513, 515.

FATHERS

By sitting late over Greek print in a badly lighted library, I finished my eyes and Schools together. I was forbidden to read for three months. Not read for three months? What was I to do? "Look," said my father, "the fence round the garden is falling to pieces, we'll replace it. We'll do it in oak: and we won't buy the uprights ready slotted, we'll cut them out with hand tools." So we made that solid oak paling right round the garden, my father and I. I wonder whether it still stands? The weeks flew by, the long sunshiny days of satisfying manual labour. I never had a happier summer than that summer I was supposed to be blind. There was the pleasure of doing a great work, and overcoming hourly difficulties. But above all, there was the pleasure of working with my father, who did not make himself the boss—he accepted me as an equal. All the time there was the feeling of his kindness, who had undertaken such a labour to keep me cheerful; but there was nothing indebting in it, it was so obvious he enjoyed the work as much as I did. My zest, however great, could not equal his. . . .

I know that it is all very well for me to go on like this, but that there may be no answering recollection in my audience—some of you don't have much to do with your fathers, and some of you wish you had less to do with them than you have. . . .

I do hope that those of you who are having a sticky passage with your fathers, and have not got over the very necessary but painful business of achieving independence from paternal tyranny, will do all you can to reestablish relations on a basis of equality as soon as possible. Do it, while the going is good: you will not have your fathers always. When my present College was so kind as to suggest my coming into it, how I should have liked to talk to my father about it, but alas!

Do you ever write to your fathers? It is an amiable and can even be an enjoyable exercise. There is a special reason. God has made known to us the mysteries of his kindness through human parables. But what makes these parables so forcible, is that they are not merely parables we can grasp, but parables we must enact. That is why they get right in amongst us. He has given us the friendship of Father and Son, on a level of equality—*nihil in hac Trinitate vel maius vel minus*—as the clue to the most august of mysteries, the life of the Godhead. It is hard for us to worship the divine reality, if we are falsifying in our own person the human parable: if we are ungrateful or indifferent sons to our earthly fathers. I am so sorry for those of you who have to try to be otherwise; I never had to try at all. My little blind soul, nosing its way into the world, had been so careful in the choice of a father.

FARRER, *THE END OF MAN*, 67–69.

MOTHERS

My sisters and I were born in Hampstead, and were brought up by a mother who was so dependable, she was almost like a piece of God's nature herself. The house always went smoothly. There was very little money behind it, but somehow no one was allowed to feel the strain. There were always good meals on time—my mother got very tired, I believe, but she did it somehow. She soothed everyone's troubles and never mentioned her own. If she had made more fuss, I suppose I should have taken more notice: if I had had to do without her, I should have seen what I owed to her. Her goodness made me thoughtless. I remember once thinking it would be fun to drive home from Oxford with three fellow students, who were going far and so wanted to start very early. "We'll stop at our place," I said, "and have breakfast." I rang my mother up at some terrible hour in the morning and we all landed hungry on the mat. The breakfast was there and my mother smiled. It was only years afterwards that she recalled the occasion, and laughed at me for having been so absurd. She had had practically nothing in the larder.

And so it is the faithfulness of God, his unseen dependableness, which makes us ungrateful. "Ah, my dear Mother," I can now say, "how I wish . . ."—but it is too late. . . .

My mother was a good woman—no one more truly a Christian—and I dare say she did not specially want to be made a fuss of, or to hear endless speeches of thanks. She wanted her children to grow and thrive on her kindness, to work along with her efforts in bringing us up. There is a sort of unthankfulness which is far more cruel than an unthankful tongue—and that is, a contempt for people's services to us. Is a cook more hurt by our lack of praise, or by our leaving her food uneaten? The worst ungratefulness to parents is, not asking for their help, not taking their advice; if they give us presents of clothes, not wearing them; if they give us presents of books, not reading them.

So it is with God. The real unthankfulness is pushing away the things he wants to give us most. We accept the material benefits—the sunshine, the rain, the food, and all the powers of nature which he has taught us to use so skilfully. And certainly God wants to give us these things, and loves to see us enjoy them, just as our mother liked to see us eat. For all our happiness is dear to God, and especially if we share it with others and invite them to our table.

But there are things he wants even more to give us—so much so, that he sent his Son to die for us. He wants to give us—how can I say it?—he wants to give us himself. Sunshine and rain, food, drink and medicine will not keep us alive for more than some seventy or eighty years. If God shares his life with us, it will keep us alive for ever. But only if the life of God gets under our skins, and makes us divine. We have to grow together into one with Christ, for God is in Christ already. . . .

Religion is all concerned with the faithfulness of God and with the unfaithfulness of men. We lose heart in religion, because we think we can trust ourselves to be faithful to God. We break down and then we are discouraged. No, religion is not pretending to be faithful, it is trust in the faithfulness of God, and going back to him again and again and again for forgiveness and a fresh start.

So, then, we have come here to thank God for his goodness. But there is only one sort of thanks he cares for, and that is, that we should use his most precious gifts, and not despise what he died to give us. "I've been dying to get to know you," people sometimes say to a new acquaintance, and heaven knows what they mean. But Christ died to get to know us, or (since he knows us already) he died to bring us into fellowship with him. "Behold," he says, "I stand at the door and knock. If any man will open, I will come in, and share his supper: and he shall share mine" [Rev 3:20].

FARRER, *THE END OF MAN*, 54–56.

CHRIST COMES TO YOU

He [Christ] may come to you in many ways. In ways in which the world would never recognize Him—in which perhaps neither you nor I shall recognize Him; but it will be enough, I hope, if we but hear His message, and obey His gracious inspiration, let Him speak through whatever means He will. He may come to us, by some crisis in our life, either for sorrow or for bliss. He may come to us by a great failure; by a great disappointment—to teach the wilful and ambitious soul, that not in *that* direction lies the path of peace. He may come in some unexpected happiness to teach that same soul that He is able and willing to give abundantly beyond all that we can ask or think. . . . He may come to us, when we are fierce and prejudiced, with that still small voice—so sweet and yet so keen. "Understand those who misunderstand thee. Be fair to those who are unfair to thee. Be just and merciful to those whom thou wouldst like to hate. Forgive, and thou shall be forgiven." He comes to us surely, when we are selfish and luxurious, in every sufferer who needs our help, and says, "If you do good to one of these, My brethren, you do it unto Me." But most surely does Christ come to us, and often most happily, and most clearly does He speak to us—in the face of a little child. . . . Ah, let us take heed that we despise not one of these little ones, lest we despise our Lord Himself. For as often as we enter into communion with little children, so often does Christ come to us. So often, as in Judea of old, does He take a little child and set it in the midst of us, that from its simplicity, docility, and trust—the restless, the mutinous, and the ambitious may learn the things which belong to their peace—so often does He say to us, "Except ye be changed and become as this little child, ye shall in no wise enter into the Kingdom of Heaven. Take my yoke upon you and learn of Me, for I am meek and lowly of heart: and ye shall find rest unto your souls" [Matt 18:3; 11:29].

KINGSLEY, WORKS, 380–82.

THE PARENTAL TYRANT

Politicians remark that no oppression is so heavy or lasting as that which is inflicted by the perversion . . . of legal authority. The robber may be seized, and the invader repelled, whenever they are found; they who pretend no right but that of force, may by force be punished or suppressed. But when plunder bears the name of impost, and murder is perpetrated by a judicial sentence, fortitude is intimidated, and wisdom confounded; . . . the villain remains secure in the robes of the magistrate.

Equally dangerous and equally detestable are the cruelties often exercised in private families, under the venerable sanction of parental authority; the power which we are taught to honour from the first moments of reason; which is guarded from insult and violation by all that can impress awe upon the mind of man; and which therefore may wanton in cruelty without control, and trample the bounds of right with innumerable transgressions, before duty and piety will dare to seek redress, or think themselves at liberty to recur to any other means of deliverance than supplications by which insolence is elated, and tears by which cruelty is gratified.

It was for a long time imagined by the Romans, that no son could be the murderer of his father; and they had therefore no punishment appropriated to parricide. They seem likewise to have believed with equal confidence, that no father could be cruel to his child; and therefore they allowed every man the supreme judicature in his own house, and put the lives of his offspring into his hands. But experience informed them by degrees, that they determined too hastily in favour of human nature; they found that instinct and habit were not able to contend with avarice or malice; that the nearest relation might be violated; and that power, to whomsoever intrusted, might be ill employed. They were therefore obliged to supply and to change their institutions; to deter the parricide by a new law, and to transfer capital punishments from the parent to the magistrate.

There are indeed many houses which it is impossible to enter familiarly, without discovering that parents are by no means exempt from the intoxications of dominion. . . .

If in any situation the heart were inaccessible to malignity, it might be supposed to be sufficiently secured by parental relation. To have voluntarily become to any being the occasion of its existence, produces an obligation to make that existence happy. To see helpless infancy stretching out her hands, and pouring out her cries in testimony of dependence, without any powers to alarm jealousy, or any guilt to alienate affection, must surely awaken tenderness in every human mind; and tenderness once excited will be hourly increased by the natural contagion of felicity, by the repercussion of communicated pleasure, by the consciousness of the dignity of benefaction. . . .

There is, indeed, another method by which the pride of superiority may be likewise gratified. He that has extinguished all the sensations of humanity, and has no longer any satisfaction in the reflection that he is loved as the distributor of happiness, may please himself with exciting terror as the inflictor of pain: he may delight his solitude with contemplating the extent of his power and the force of his commands; in imagining the desires that flutter on the tongue which is forbidden to utter them, or the discontent which preys on the heart in which fear confines it; he may amuse himself with new contrivances of detection, multiplications of prohibition, and varieties of punishment. . . .

. . . The regal and parental tyrants differ only in the extent of their dominions, and the number of their slaves. The same passions cause the same miseries; except that seldom any prince, however despotic, has so far shaken off all awe of the public eye, as to venture upon those freaks of injustice, which are sometimes indulged under the secrecy of a private dwelling. Capricious injunctions, partial decisions, unequal allotments, distributions of reward, not by merit, but by fancy, and punishments, regulated not by the degree of the offence, but by the humour of the judge, are too frequent where no power is known but that of a father. . . .

[W]hat can a parent hope from the oppression of those who were born to his protection, of those who can disturb him with no competition, who can enrich him with no spoils? Why cowards are cruel may be easily discovered; but for what reason, not more infamous than cowardice, can that man delight in oppression who has nothing to fear?

The unjustifiable severity of a parent is loaded with this aggravation, that those whom he injures are always in his sight. The injustice of a prince is often exercised upon those of whom he never had any personal or particular knowledge; and the sentence which he pronounces, whether of banishment, imprisonment, or death, removes from his view the man whom he condemns. But the domestic oppressor dooms himself to gaze upon those faces which he clouds with terror and with sorrow; and beholds every moment the effects of his own barbarities. He that can bear to give continual pain to those who surround him, and can walk with satisfaction in the gloom of his own presence; he that can see submissive misery without relenting, and meet without emotion the eye that implores mercy or demands justice, will scarcely be amended by remonstrance or admonition; he has found means of stopping the avenues of tenderness, and arming his heart against the force of reason. . . .

Every man, however little he loves others, would willingly be loved; every man hopes to live long. . . . [There may come a time in old age when he] must depend for ease and cheerfulness upon . . . others. But how has he obviated the inconveniences of old age, who alienates from him the assistance of his children, and whose bed must be surrounded in the last hours, in the hours of languor and dejection, of impatience and pain, by strangers to whom his life is indifferent, or by enemies to whom his death is desirable?

Piety will indeed in good minds overcome provocation, and those who have been harassed by brutality will forget the injuries which they have suffered, so far as to perform the last duties with alacrity and zeal. But surely no resentment can be equally painful with kindness thus undeserved, nor can severer punishment be imprecated upon a man not wholly lost in meanness and stupidity, than through the tediousness of decrepitude, to be reproached by the kindness of his own children, to receive not the tribute but the alms of attendance, and to owe every relief of his miseries, not to gratitude but to mercy.

JOHNSON, *THE RAMBLER* (NO. 148), 228–29.

PATIENT AND LOVING

If "the child is father of the man," *we should be patient with him.* How much we need God's patience! How we try it! How it still waits upon us. And how impatient we are apt to be with children. We forget that we ourselves were children once. We forget how wayward we were then; how disobedient, how rebellious. Nay, that we are still so, toward God. And that their faults, it may be, are but the reflections of our own. A child is a tender thing. It must be handled tenderly. A rough word may break down its spirit. A sneer may embitter it, for life. A rude touch may set it wrong, for eternity. God developes His own handiwork, in time.

If "the child is father of the man," *we should be loving with him.* Love is the universal solvent. God does nothing without love. Man can do nothing but by it. Machinery is moved by power. Hearts must be swayed by love. It is so especially with children. Hence the instinctive love with which a newborn babe is welcomed into life. Hence the attractiveness of little children. But it must be more than this. They are not always lovely. And yet we must be always loving. And the less loveliness, the more love. Only love can exercise the watchfulness which little children call for. Only love can prompt the perpetual hopefulness. Only love sustain the unwearying patience. Nor is it a weak, blind love that meets the case. "Whom the Lord loveth he chasteneth" [Heb 12:6]. And it must be so with children. Nothing . . . taxes love like the faults which call for chastisement. Nothing . . . tries love like the decision to administer it. Nothing . . . *grieves* love like its administration. . . . When God would set forth His love with an argument which all can understand and none can resist, the appeal is to the paternal instinct: "As a father pitieth his own children, even so is the Lord merciful to them that fear Him" [Ps 103:13].

DOANE, *LIFE AND WRITINGS* 4:62–63.

AN ICON FOR CHRISTMAS

If I look for an icon for Christmas, what I see is a mother and child and the radiant love between them—not necessarily Mary, the mother of God, but any one of us human mothers holding our babe in delight and joy.

This icon, too, alas, can become idol. When a mother manipulates, controls, abuses, ignores, dominates, sees her own motherhood as more important than the child she has birthed, idolatry is again rampant.

But the icon can remain clear even when we make mistakes, as all mothers do. We are human creatures, and with the best will in the world we do the wrong things. But as long as we remember that creation, including our children, is God's, not ours, the icon of mother and child can be an open window.

God created, and looked on Creation, and cried out, "It is good!"

L'ENGLE, "CHRISTMAS," 2.

PRACTICE IN FREEDOM

[T]he parent . . . needs practice in freedom quite as much as the child does. It is perhaps here, more than anywhere else, that the inordinate need of some parents for their children takes its toll. . . . There is no worse burden to load on a child's shoulders than the unspoken sense that his parents are dependent on him, must possess him, and must continually sap and draw his strength to meet their necessities. It is necessary for the child's exercise of freedom that he understand that his parents are free from him, and are, therefore, competent to lead him truly . . . into the ever wider world of his increasingly mature choices. No one is quicker than a child to sense a wrong interpretation of freedom, or a guidance which is misleading because it is egocentric on the parent's part. . . .

For there is little in a child's life which bothers and torments him more than the feeling that he is the center of his parents' world. He has no business being father and mother to them—he is going to have children of his own, sometime, to love and guide; and it is for the coming generation that God gave him his own parental instincts. Therefore, every child responds well and happily in the knowledge that his parents have their own life, and are pleased and successful in living it.

BAYNE, CHRISTIAN LIVING, 102–3.

THE BEGINNING OF WISDOM

Many of the behavioral and personality traits of my dog ["Mark"]—as those of any human being—remain a mystery, however much I may try to understand them. Recognizing this fact does, I suppose, represent the beginning of wisdom.

Mark's mature personality is neither wholly what I expected it to be nor exactly what I would desire. I have never known any living creature to develop just as I thought he or she should. Nearly always I have expected too much; however, in my better moments I have realized that what I expected was not nearly as fine as what developed. . . .

Like human beings, dogs grow to be uniquely themselves—a composite of their genes and of those with whom they associate. Occasionally those selves are greater than the dreams their masters have for them, but those selves are always different. This is as it should be. Fortunately we cannot make, or remake, dogs or [children]. We can but cooperate with One who knows more about making and remaking than we do.

MARTIN, *LETTERS*, 99–100, 103–4.

13

Friendship

FRIENDSHIP AND HEAVEN

Those who cannot conceive Friendship as a substantive love but only as a disguise or elaboration of Eros betray the fact that they have never had a Friend. The rest of us know that though we can have erotic love and friendship for the same person yet in some ways nothing is less like a Friendship than a love-affair. Lovers are always talking to one another about their love; Friends hardly ever about their Friendship. Lovers are normally face to face, absorbed in each other; Friends, side by side, absorbed in some common interest. Above all, Eros (while it lasts) is necessarily between two only. But two, far from being the necessary number for Friendship, is not even the best. And the reason for this is important. . . .

In each of my friends there is something that only some other friend can fully bring out. By myself I am not large enough to call the whole man into activity: I want other lights than my own to show all his facets. Now that Charles is dead, I shall never again see Ronald's reaction to a specifically Caroline joke. Far from having more of Ronald, having him "to myself" now that Charles is away, I have less of Ronald. Hence true Friendship is the least jealous of loves. Two friends delight to be joined by a third, and three by a fourth, if only the newcomer is qualified to become a real friend. They can then say, as the blessed souls say in Dante, "Here comes one who will augment our loves." For in this love "to divide is not to take away."

In this, Friendship exhibits a glorious "nearness by resemblance" to Heaven itself where the very multitude of the blessed (which no man can number) increases the fruition which each has of God. For every soul, seeing Him in her own way, doubtless communicates that unique vision to all the rest. That, says an old author, is why the Seraphim in Isaiah's vision are crying "Holy, Holy, Holy" *to one another* [Isa 6:3]. The more we thus share the Heavenly Bread between us, the more we shall all have.

LEWIS, *THE FOUR LOVES*, 91–93.

FRIENDSHIP AND PRIDE

The danger of . . . pride is . . . almost inseparable from Friendly love. Friendship must exclude. From the innocent and necessary act of excluding to the spirit of exclusiveness is an easy step; and thence to the degrading pleasure of exclusiveness. If that is once admitted the downward slope will grow rapidly steeper. . . .

The common vision which first brought us together may fade quite away. We shall be a *coterie* that exists for the sake of being a *coterie*; a little self-elected (and therefore absurd) aristocracy, basking in the moonshine of our collective self-approval. . . .

The mass of the people, who are never quite right, are never quite wrong. They are hopelessly mistaken in their belief that every knot of friends came into existence for the sake of the pleasures of conceit and superiority. They are, I trust, mistaken in their belief that every Friendship actually indulges in these pleasures. But they would seem to be right in diagnosing pride as the danger to which Friendships are naturally liable. Just because this is the most spiritual of loves the danger which besets it is spiritual too. Friendship is even, if you like, angelic. But man needs to be triply protected by humility if he is to eat the bread of angels without risk.

LEWIS, *THE FOUR LOVES*, 122, 123–24.

IN CIRCLES

The occasions for kindness ring us round in two circles. The inner circle is made up of our ordinary environment. How do you view the people among whom you move? Are you going to cultivate the successful and neglect the less attractive . . . ? Are you ever going to ask, who needs friendship most? Of course there is a special place for our most congenial friends; it is another thing, if we shutter our minds against others, or close our doors.

So much for the inner circle of kindness, which touches us all the time; so surely it concerns us most. But then there is the outer circle, most distant, hungry and dark—the needs of those less privileged than we are.

FARRER, *THE BRINK OF MYSTERY*, 55.

TRUE FRIENDSHIP

We are often, by superficial accomplishments and accidental endearments, induced to love those whom we cannot esteem; we are sometimes, by great abilities and incontestable evidences of virtue, compelled to esteem those whom we cannot love. But friendship, compounded of esteem and love, derives from one its tenderness, and its permanence from the other; and therefore requires not only that its candidates should gain the judgement, but that they should attract the affections; that they should not only be firm in the day of distress, but gay in the hour of jollity; not only useful in exigences, but pleasing in familiar life; their presence should give cheerfulness as well as courage, and dispel alike the gloom of fear and of melancholy.

JOHNSON, *THE RAMBLER* (NO. 64), 107.

THE SPIRITUAL REALITY OF FRIENDSHIP

One of the most completely satisfying things in life is friendship. In any deep sense it is one of the rarest things. Pure and deep love is easier found than pure and deep friendship. We all have friends, of course, in some limited and partial sense: persons with whom we are intimate, and in whose company we take pleasure. We are sorry to separate from them; we remember them with gratitude. But friendship in the full meaning of the word is other than that. It is founded in some subtle sympathy of nature. It brings about a complete frankness of intercourse; an *abandon* by virtue of which one can appear perfectly natural to another, and can to another reveal the very soul. Its essence would seem to be an instinctive mutual understanding, so complete that there needs no explanation. One is secure in revealing oneself, for one is certain of not being misunderstood. Love is founded other where; and one of its limitations is that it does not remove misunderstanding. It is founded in passion, not sympathy. But friendship is perfected in sympathy. It gives nature an outlet; it enables us to show ourselves to another, without fear of that other's criticism. While we dread criticism in general, we court the criticism of friends. We are willing to talk frankly and without defense of our failings, secure that we shall be told the truth; secure that we shall be told the truth in love.

This human friendship, so rare, so perfect, is but the adumbration of a more perfect thing. Most human relations are the shadows of spiritual realities; they find their full significance in the relation of the soul to God. You remember that . . . passage in St. John, where our Lord says to His Apostles: "Henceforth I call you not servants, but I have called you friends" [John 15:15]. What a wonderful glimpse there is there into our possible relation to God.

Barry, Meditations on the Holy Spirit, 181–83.

GOD SANCTIFIES FRIENDSHIP

Hearts are linked to hearts by God. The friend on whose fidelity you count, whose success in life flushes your cheek with honest satisfaction, whose triumphant career you have traced and read with a heart throbbing almost as if it were a thing alive, for whose honor you would answer as for your own,—that friend, given to you by circumstances over which you had no control, was God's own gift.

Robertson, Living Thoughts, 86.

HUMAN FELLOWSHIP

Much becomes clear to us when we learn that God wishes to raise and educate our *wills*; that there is no love but what is kindled in them, but what is kept alive in them, by His Holy Spirit. Then we find that the exhortation to stir up that Spirit within us is an exhortation which can be followed, because we are never alone in our efforts, because when we are thinking the best thoughts, forming our best resolves, we are only thinking what He is working in us to think, resolving what He inspires us to resolve. And is it not true also . . . that this Spirit is with us to guide our social intercourse, to draw forth out of us those deep inward convictions and heart-utterances which really answer to one another, to make our words real and not mocking words, to change us from scoffing critics into human beings? Shall not a body of men acquainted with each other, helping each other to fight, sustaining each other in falls, holding forth to each other the prize of a common victory, be possible once more on earth? Are we to live in an age in which every mechanical facility for communication between man and man is multiplied ten-thousandfold, only that the inward isolation, the separation of those who meet continually, may be increased in a far greater measure? Is this to be the final reward of civilisation, that instead of human faces there are to be only grinning masks, lumps of ice for beating hearts? May not . . . a communion exist which shall answer to the name, a communion of men united by holy sacraments of affection to each other, because of service and devotion to Christ and to those for whom He died?

MAURICE, LESSONS OF HOPE, 101–3.

14

Human Beings and Nature

GOD THE AUTHOR OF NATURE

I worship the God of beauty. Human skill, I tell myself, is proud to have arranged a single pattern of aesthetic charm on a few feet of painted canvas; divine contrivance has set a whole landscape in everlasting rock, in rushing torrents and in springing trees. And in telling myself this I do not err. That adaptation of my eye to environment and of environment to my eye, which produces aesthetic delight, is a masterpiece of God's skill. Not only has he created man, he has fitted him to his environment in a hundred subtle ways; among which not the least remarkable is this relation of things to our eye, giving aesthetic delight, and sometimes ecstasy.

Only I must beware of over-humanising or of taking the comparison between God and the painter too far. The painter thinks of nothing but the picture. He is interested in the paint and canvas solely for the way they can be made to look. What their chemical composition may be, what active processes are going on in the atoms that make them up, is of no concern to him. He is merely careful to select materials which will place no obstacles in his way, nor do anything to cramp his liberty in painting. If then I allow myself to think of God as an artist in living landscape, I shall wonder why he uses materials which are so largely irrelevant to his purpose, so frustrating; and I shall notice that, while some of his works are supremely beautiful, some are humdrum to the eye, some hideous and discordant; as though his materials had got out of hand and defeated his artistry.

What is my mistake? I have forgotten that God is the Cause of the world's existence, and that he has woven nature up from the bottom. That

natural beauty which is such a charm in my eyes is, as it were, a divine af-
terthought; a sweet enjoyment for mankind in the look of a world whose
existence serves quite other ends. Scenic beauty belongs to the sphere of
man, and man was a late arrival. The masses of the mountains were not
trimmed for human eyes; landscape is not a landscape-garden. God's
goodness is not disappointed because not all scenes are equally lovely to
us. God does not form ideal projects and regret to find them imperfectly
realizable. He rejoices that rocks and trees, rivers and meadows, created
on quite other principles, afford such feasts to human eyes.

FARRER, *GOD IS NOT DEAD*, 72–74.

A REASONABLE CREATURE

With regard to what God can or cannot do, we ought always to think and
speak with the greatest humility, with a due sense of our own ignorance,
and of the infinite perfections of the divine nature. God is almighty, that
is, he can do every thing: and yet he can do nothing, the doing of which
implies a contradiction in itself, or to his own holy nature. We hesitate
not to say, that God cannot make a thing *to be* and *not to be*, at the same
time; or to be both true and false under the same circumstances; because,
being and *not being*, *truth* and *falsehood* contradict and mutually destroy
each other. Again; we say without scruple, that God cannot deny himself,
or speak, or act falsely; because, to do so would be against the truth and
holiness of his own nature. However almighty and absolute, therefore, the
power of God over his creatures may be, it will always be exerted according to their nature; because their nature is his gift; and his having given a
particular nature to certain creatures is an implied promise and assurance,
as strong as words could make it, that he will deal with them according to
that particular nature which he hath given them, and not according to another nature which belongs not to them. . . . Through the whole Bible, man
is considered as a reasonable creature; having ability to regard the motions
of God's Spirit, or to reject them; to turn himself to them, or from them;
to comply with them, or to quench them; that is, as having a Will of his
own, and the power of determining his own actions; and not as being the
subject of irresistible compulsion. On no other ground can we reconcile it
with the goodness or justice of God, that men should be left to live in error
and delusion, corrupting one another, and perverting the plain doctrines
of the Gospel; or in vice and villainy, in opposition to the laws of God and
man. For if God can, consistently with his own nature and the nature of

man, change the human heart by his absolute over-ruling power, it might be done for all men, and then all men might be made *good*, whenever God pleased. In this way, error and delusion, sin and wickedness, vice and villainy, and every thing that is evil in man, might be taken away. God is infinite in goodness and holiness: Why then is not this done? Because man has a *will* of his own, and cannot be made good, or holy, or happy in opposition to it.

SEABURY, DISCOURSES, 265–66, 268.

ANIMALS

Listen to the poets of Israel: "Oh God, thou preservest man and beast." "The eyes of all wait upon thee." "He causeth grass to grow for the cattle." "The high hills are a refuge for the wild goats, and the rocks for the conies." And then there is that superb outburst of music which closes the whole psalter and calls upon "everything that hath breath" to "praise the Lord." Among the prophets of Israel we note that Isaiah bids his people learn lessons from the ox and the ass. Balaam is rebuked for striking the animal on which he rode. Jonah is reproved for his inhumanity in failing to consider not only the children but the cattle which would be included in the judgment that he invoked on the city of Nineveh. So our Lord Jesus Christ was fulfilling the best traditions of his people when he showed his sympathy with the foxes who had holes and the birds that had nests, and when he said that, though five sparrows were sold for a farthing, not one of them fell to the ground without the Father's knowledge. He compared, you remember, his own love for the people of Jerusalem with that of a mother hen gathering her chickens under her wings. . . .

[People] can be sentimental and silly about animals, but it is a fact that we are bound up with the animals in God's creation. We depend on them and they depend on us. They are at our mercy. . . . The very power we have over them entitles them to our care and protection as children are entitled to the care and protection of their parents. As Browning said:

> *God made all creatures and gave them our love and our fear,*
> *To give sign, we and they are his children, one family here.*

. . . Care and compassion for animals has a way of clearing the channels of communication with God.

> *He prayeth best who loveth best*
> *All creatures great and small.*

"Blessed are the merciful, for they shall obtain mercy" [Matt 5:7]. Many good men have indeed had their thoughts turned and raised to God by contemplating the animals and in consequence have taken part with more fervour in the worship of God. John Keble wrote a poem "To a thrush singing in January":

> *Sweet bird, up earliest in the morn,*
> *Up earliest in the year,*
> *Far in the quiet mist are borne*
> *Thy matins soft and clear.*

For these and all his mercies God's holy name be praised.

VIDLER, *WINDSOR SERMONS*, 174–76.

LOVING THE CREATED ORDER

I will never laugh at anyone for grieving over a loved beast. I think God wants us to love Him more, not to love creatures (even animals) less. We love everything in one way too much (i.e. at the expense of our love for Him) but in another way we love everything too little.

No person, animal, flower, or even pebble has ever been loved too much—i.e. more than every one of God's works deserves.

LEWIS, *LETTERS TO AN AMERICAN LADY*, 58.

THE CIRCLE OF PAST AND FUTURE

It seems to me that a certain rhythm, a certain balance of continuity with change, is what one needs for a sane and reasonable life. Nature provides the model. Day and night follow each other in an unbroken order, and the yearly cycle of the seasons never fails. Yet each day is a little different, and every so often one day is very different.

The pattern of nature has been followed in the liturgy. Daily Morning and Evening Prayer follow the same pattern day after day, while psalms, lessons, and other items within that pattern vary. The Holy Eucharist generally adheres to the same framework every Sunday, but again specific items within the pattern vary. Occasionally, there are very special days which break the pattern, but there are few such days in a year. This is a good pace for human living.

Yet one cannot end the discussion there. All of us hope for something more, either for ourselves or for those whom we love, beyond the mere repetition of calm days, weeks, and years. It is a real question, how much or how little to hope for in this life. Those who hope for too much, risk grave disappointment. Those who hope for too little will easily be passed by.

PORTER, *A SONG OF CREATION*, 83.

THE SUN COMING FORTH

The first article of the Christian faith, our belief in God as the maker and creator of all things, affects our view of anything and everything. It is not easy to picture God existing by himself from all eternity, beginning to make everything out of nothing. Nor is it easy to picture any alternatives. To imagine that everything which now is has been from all eternity, this is also to dumbfound the mind. Neither poetic imagination, nor common sense, nor the science of physics find it congenial to speak of an ever-existing universe. Neither is it easy to join our atheist friends and suppose that everything just happened to come into existence because of an accident. It is hard to picture an accident occurring before there is anything to have it!

For our ancestors long ago, and for our spiritual forebears who wrote the Bible, it was also difficult to picture how everything came into existence at the dawn of time. For them, as for us, it was helpful to consider those entries into existence which we ourselves can see or feel. The most obvious personal experience of something like creation is the return of day every 24 hours. This is one of the most characteristic events on the surface of this planet. After the deathlike non-consciousness of sleep, we awake, we find ourselves alive again, and we enter a new day. If we awake early enough, we will see the dawn. After the darkness of night, a gray twilight comes first. The dawn wind stirs. The shapes of clouds become visible. Soon we can see the face of the earth spread out, and trees, bushes, buildings, and bodies of water appear. The sun itself emerges above the horizon in glory. Birds are noisy, and if we live in the country, we will hear other animals too. In due course we ourselves, the last created, emerge onto the scene.

> Man goes forth to his work
> and to his labor until the evening. [Ps 104:24]

. . . To reflect upon the Bible, to enter into the sacred history, to go through the threshold which it opens to us—to do this requires a certain give-and-take, a thoughtful and reflective exchange between our life and experiences, and the words of the Scriptures. As we do this, we discover that things are indeed made new, we are made new, and we catch a glimpse, we feel a throbbing, we hear a whisper of the meaning of that ongoing mystery of the creative power of God.

PORTER, *A SONG OF CREATION*, 73–74.

THE SPRING OF LIFE

There is, I believe, scarce any poet of eminence, who has not left some testimony of his fondness for the flowers, the zephyrs, and the warblers of the spring. Nor has the most luxuriant imagination been able to describe serenity and happiness of the golden age, otherwise than by giving a perpetual spring, as the highest reward of uncorrupted innocence.

There is, indeed, something inexpressibly pleasing, in the annual renovation of the world, and the new display of the treasures of nature. The cold and darkness of winter, with the naked deformity of every object on which we turn our eyes, makes us rejoice at the succeeding season, as well for what we have escaped, as for what we may enjoy; and every budding flower, which a warm situation brings early to our view, is considered by us as a messenger to notify the approach of more joyous days.

The Spring affords to a mind, so free from the disturbance of cares or passions as to be vacant to calm amusements, almost every thing that our present state makes us capable of enjoying. The variegated verdure of the fields and woods, the succession of grateful odours, the voice of pleasure pouring out its notes on every side, with the gladness apparently conceived by every animal, from the growth of his food, and the clemency of the weather, throw over the whole earth an air of gayety, significantly expressed by the smile of nature.

Yet there are men to whom these scenes are able to give no delight, and who hurry away from all the varieties of rural beauty, to lose their hours, and divert their thoughts by cards, or assemblies, a tavern dinner, or the prattle of the day. . . .

He that enlarges his curiosity after the works of nature, demonstrably multiplies the inlets to happiness; and, therefore, the younger part of my readers, to whom I dedicate this vernal speculation, must excuse me for calling upon them, to make use at once of the spring of the year, and the spring of life; to acquire, while their minds may be yet impressed with new images, a love of innocent pleasures, and an ardour for useful knowledge; and to remember, that a blighted spring makes a barren year, and that the vernal flowers, however beautiful and gay, are only intended by nature as preparatives to autumnal fruits.

JOHNSON, *THE RAMBLER* (NO. 5), 19–20.

GOD'S GREAT GREEN BOOK

By looking upon this beautiful . . . world around us with reverence, and earnestness, and love, . . . we shall become not merely the more learned, or the more happy, we shall become . . . better men. The beauties in the earth and sky; the flowers with their fair hues and fragrant scents; the song birds; the green shaughs [thickets] and woodlands; the moors purple with heath, and golden with furze [evergreen shrubs]; the shapes of clouds, from the delicate mist upon the lawn to the thunder pillar towering up in awful might; the sunrise and sunset, painted by God afresh each morn and even; the blue sky, which is the image of God the heavenly Father, boundless, clear and calm, looking down on all below with the same smile of love, sending his rain alike on the evil and on the good, and causing his sun to shine alike on the just and on the unjust:— he who watches all these things, day by day, will find his heart grow quiet, sober, meek, contented. His eyes will be turned away from beholding vanity. His soul will be kept from vexation of spirit. In God's tabernacle, which is the universe of all the worlds, lie will be kept from the strife of tongues. As he watches the work of God's Spirit, the beauty of God's Spirit, the wisdom of God's Spirit, the fruitfulness of God's Spirit, which shines forth in every wayside flower, and every gnat which dances in the sun, he will rejoice in God's works, even as God himself rejoices. He will learn to value things at their true price, and see things of their real size. Ambition, fame, money, will seem small things to him as he considers the lilies of the field, how the heavenly Father clothes them, and the birds of the air, how the heavenly Father feeds them.

KINGSLEY, *DISCIPLINE*, 244–45.

15

Toward the Abundant Life

FELLOW WORKERS

The love of God must be accompanied by love to man. If we realize God as our Father, we must love the brethren for our Father's sake. If we realize the goodness of God's gifts as derived from the Giver, and not inherent in themselves, we must feel their only value to consist in using them according to God's will, for the benefit of our brethren, and to the praise of his glory. A true love of God, therefore, cannot withhold what God has given, for it is due to our brethren, since we are but stewards of our common Father's property; and if it is withholden it ceases to be good, for the goodness of the Giver passes away: and what is good as the instrument of His energy is but a curse as the mere possession of our selfishness. What privilege can be so great to those who love God as the privilege of being fellow-workers with Him? If God is really loved, we cannot value any worldly power in itself, but merely in so far as we can make evident His energy within us, in its use for the purposes of love.

BENSON, *WISDOM*, 124–25.

TO STAND ALONE

One of the great powers of character is the power to stand alone. One feels sure that many of the failures of the moral and spiritual life are due to the lack of that power—the ability to stand out against criticism, against the silent pressure of example, against the constant pull of our social environment. If therefore one has got into a social environment that is unsympathetic with one's aims and ideals, one finds one's position by no means easy or pleasant. Unless one has great determination of character one is almost certain to be spiritually debilitated by the unwholesome atmosphere in which one lives. Most people have little determination and are quickly responsive to the nearest influence. Society is filled with people of no moral stamina; people who mean well and want, on the whole, to serve God, but who actually do not effectively serve him but are given over to the world. They are moral jelly-fish ready to take any shape that the society they find themselves in demands. They gradually lapse from the Christian standard of the Will of God to the worldly standard of what other people do. The pity of it is that they so rarely understand what they have done. They consider that occasional compliance with the externals of religion is the equivalent of a Christian life and a Christian service.

BARRY, THE CHRISTIAN DAY, 144–45.

THANKSGIVING

We feel . . . how hard it is to keep any vigor of thankfulness unless there be upon us the stress of a present deliverance. We find it difficult to keep clear to us the ever-present goodness of God in the daily deliverance of our lives. Yet it is there, the mercy of God. It is there, the basis and the obligation of thankfulness which we do ill to neglect. . . . The Church . . . makes thanksgiving a constant element of *worship*. That the Christian Church makes thanksgiving a part of all daily offices shows the value attached to the virtue, and the emphasis. And then, surely, it is suggestive that the one divinely instituted act of worship bears the name Eucharist, Thanksgiving. . . .

But first, let us recall what thankfulness is. It is not an impulsive emotion, called out by an exceptional occurrence or passing event. The emotion of gratitude which we feel in some *unusual* situation is well enough, but it is not the virtue of gratitude. Thankfulness, as a Christian virtue, is a permanent attitude of soul, founded on due consideration of facts. It is the answer by man, to God's dealing with his *whole* life. There is a decided difference between the vivid emotion we feel at the gratification of some wish, or the escape from some danger, and the steady perpetual gratification we feel towards God for "all his goodness and loving kindness" which finds expression in what he *denies* as in what he gives. . . .

Things may be great blessings to us, which are not at all pleasures. . . . We talk about blessings in disguise, but are not anxious to have them come that way. And yet, in the wisdom of God, that is often the best way. Perhaps God sees that the deeper blessings of the life of love and union can be ours only as the way is cut for them through the selfishness or worldliness or hardness of our lives.

BARRY, *THE CHRISTIAN DAY*, 247–48, 244–45, 255.

THE DUTY OF THANKSGIVING

The duty of offering thanksgiving and praise to Almighty God results from the acknowledgment of his being, his attributes, and his providence. To believe in his existence, and not to adore him who is the glorious fountain of being; to acknowledge that he is infinite in power, in wisdom, in justice, in holiness, in goodness, and in mercy, and yet not to render him homage for his great and glorious attributes; to behold him ruling over all, opening his hand and filling all things with good, and yet to be silent and insensible when his mercies are dispensed to us, would be contrary to the dictates of reason and the feelings of nature.

The Almighty Being who governs in righteousness the universe, which is the work of his hands, who is God over all, blessed for evermore, claims our homage, from the excellence of his character and the supremacy of his power. The powers of our minds discern and acknowledge the charms of moral perfection; our hearts are warmed by the displays of exalted goodness; an ingenuous sentiment of nature always impels us to thank the benefactor who loads us with favours; surely, then, the offering of homage to him who is the glorious source of all perfection, the centre of all goodness, and all-gracious Benefactor of the universe, will be a dictate of reason and an impulse of the heart. "It is good to sing praises unto God; it is pleasant; and praise is comely" [Ps 147:1].

Why were we made capable of knowing the infinite and eternal source from which all our blessings flow? Why does revelation assure us, and reason confirm the truth, that we are indebted to a superior power for all the enjoyments of life, even to that Almighty Being who is the Author of every good and perfect gift? There is no sentiment of the human heart which is not designed by our all-wise Creator for some useful and beneficent end; and for what purpose could the sentiment of dependence, so deeply seated in our nature, be designed, but to prompt us not only to supplicate the bounty, but to praise the goodness of that Almighty Benefactor who dispenses to us all our blessings? In those moments of difficulty and danger, when bowed down by affliction and depressed by sickness, when assailed by the malice of our enemies, and deserted by our faithless friends, to whom does an irresistible sentiment of nature urge us to flee, but to that infinitely gracious Being who is the guardian of the oppressed, and the refuge of the miserable? And shall we implore his succour, and yet be insensible to his goodness? Shall we experience his mercy, and yet refuse to render him the tribute of praise? Selfish and degraded indeed is man's nature, if, while it prompts him to flee to the throne of the Almighty in the hour of danger, it does not also excite him, in the season of deliverance, to bless that gracious Being who redeemeth his life from destruction, and crowneth him with loving-kindness and tender mercies.

There is no sentiment which is universally acknowledged as more amiable and noble than that which prompts us thankfully to acknowledge the favours which we have received, and to bless the benefactor whose disinterested exertions have been devoted to our service; and shall we generously and promptly acknowledge the favours which we have received from our fellow-men—shall we bestow veneration and gratitude on the earthly parent, whose painful watchings, whose assiduous exertions and unwearied care protected us from danger, soothed us in sickness, and surrounded us with comforts—shall we delight to blend with the emotions of affection, the feelings of gratitude to the friend of our bosoms, whose generous devotion to us has been paid at the sacrifice of his own comfort? Surely we cannot exercise these feelings towards our earthly benefactors, our earthly parents and friends, and withhold the tribute of gratitude from that heavenly Benefactor who surrounds us with good, that heavenly Parent who is the Preserver of our lives and the Father of our spirits, that Almighty Friend who sticketh closer than a brother, who will never leave us nor forsake us, not though we pass through the valley of the shadow of death.

HOBART, *THE POSTHUMOUS WORKS*, 321–23.

THY WILL BE DONE

There is a haughty spirit which though it will not complain, does not care to submit. It arrogates to itself the dignity of enduring, without any claim to the meekness of yielding. Its silence is stubbornness, its fortitude is pride; its calmness is apathy without, and discontent within. In such characters, it is not so much the will of God which is the rule of conduct, as the scorn of pusillanimity. Not seldom indeed the mind puts in a claim for a merit to which the nerves could make out a better title. . . . True resignation is the hardest lesson in the whole school of Christ. It is the oftenest taught and the latest learnt. It is not a task which, when once got over in some particular instance, leaves us master of the subject. The necessity of following up the lesson we have begun, presents itself almost every day in some new shape. . . . The submission of yesterday does not exonerate us from the resignation of to-day. . . .

Submission is a duty of such high and holy import that it can only be learnt of the Great Teacher. If it could have been acquired by mere moral institution, the wise sayings of the ancient philosophers would have taught it. . . .

We must remember, that in offering this prayer ["Thy will be done"], we may by our own request, be offering to resign what we most dread to lose, to give up what is dear to us as our own soul: we may be recalling our own Heavenly Father to withhold what we are most anxiously labouring to obtain, and to withdraw what we are most sedulously endeavouring to keep. We are most solemnly renouncing our property in ourselves, we are distinctly making ourselves over again to Him whose we already are. We specifically entreat him to do with us what he pleases, to mould us to a conformity to his image, without which we shall never be resigned to his will. In short, to dispose of us as his infinite wisdom sees best, however contrary to the scheme which our blindness has laid down as the path to unquestionable happiness.

To render this trying petition easy to us, is one great reason why God by such a variety of providences, afflicts and brings us low.

He knows we want incentives to humility, even more than incitements to virtuous actions. He shows us in many ways, that self-sufficiency and happiness are incompatible, that pride and peace are irreconcilable; that, following our own way, and doing our own will, which we consider to be the very essence of felicity, is in direct opposition to it.

MORE, *CHRISTIAN MORALS*, 131–32.

REAL RESIGNATION

Screwtape to Wormwood:

What the Enemy [God] means by this [submission to His will] is primarily that [the patient] should accept . . . the tribulation which has actually been dealt out to him—the present anxiety and suspense. It is about *this* that he is to say "Thy will be done," and for the daily task of bearing *this* that the daily bread will be provided. It is your business to see that the patient never thinks of the present fear as his appointed cross, but only of the things he is afraid of. Let him regard them as his crosses: let him forget that, since they are incompatible, they cannot all happen to him, and let him try to practise fortitude and patience to them all in advance. For real resignation, at the same moment, to a dozen different and hypothetical fates, is almost impossible, and the Enemy does not greatly assist those who are trying to attain it: resignation to present and actual suffering, even where that suffering consists of fear, is far easier, and is usually helped by this direct action.

LEWIS, *THE SCREWTAPE LETTERS*, 29.

TRUST IN GOD

Shall we reduce St. Mark's Gospel to three lines?

God gives you everything.
Give everything to God.
You can't.

True, there is a fourth line; Christ will make you able, for he has risen from the dead. But this is almost overshadowed in St. Mark's Gospel by the emphasis on self-distrust. St. Mark seems even more afraid that his readers will trust themselves than that they will distrust Christ's risen power.

Perhaps the Mark of the gospel was the John Mark of Acts after all. And perhaps all this emphasis on desertion, running away, the failure of good intentions has something to do with that most painful text in the Book of Acts: "Barnabas wished to take John called Mark with them; but Paul thought it not well to take with them him who had turned back from them in Pamphylia, and not gone with them to the work" [Acts 15:37–38]. If the Evangelist is that Mark who had once turned back, and of whom St. Paul had thought the worse for his turning back, then he had evidently learned from his turning back what God wished him to learn from it: that it is not in us to follow Christ, it is Christ's gift.

Happy is the man who learns from his own failures. He certainly won't learn from anyone else's. Here I am on safe ground, for when it comes to serving God we are all failures, are we not? So there is no fear of my missing my target in any of my readers. It is humiliating how, especially in the bosom of our families, childish faults of temper reassert themselves which we hoped we had outgrown: humiliating how, as soon as a change of scene removes the encouraging company of our Christian friends, our religion languishes. We have not prayed nor worked nor controlled ourselves as we hoped to do. God has given us much; we have not given anything worth mentioning to God. Well, St. Mark (if he is indeed the same man) went back from the work in Pamphylia, and in Gethsemane none of the disciples behaved with credit.

It is by these desolating experiences that God teaches us to trust him, not ourselves. The more emptied out we are, the more hope there is of our learning to be Christians. Now is the very moment—there will never be a better—for us to put our trust in the God who makes something from nothing, who raises the dead.

FARRER, *A FAITH OF OUR OWN*, 112–14.

INVOKING THE HOLY SPIRIT

When we pray "Come, Holy Ghost, our souls inspire," we had better know what we are about. He will not carry us to easy triumphs and gratifying successes; more probably he will set us to some task for God in the full intention that we shall fail, so that others, learning wisdom by our failure, may carry the good cause forward. He may take us through loneliness, desertion by friends, apparent desertion even by God; that was the way Christ went to the Father. He may drive us into the wilderness to be tempted of the devil. He may lead us from the Mount of Transfiguration (if he ever lets us climb it) to the hill that is called the Place of a Skull. For if we invoke him, it must be to help us in doing God's will, not ours. We cannot call upon the Creator Spirit, by whose aid The world's foundations first were laid in order to use omnipotence for the supply of our futile pleasures or the success of our futile plans. If we invoke him, we must be ready for the glorious pain of being caught by his power out of our petty orbit into the eternal purposes of the Almighty, in whose onward sweep our lives are as a speck of dust. The soul that is filled with the Spirit must have become purged of all pride or love of ease, all self-complacence and self-reliance; but that soul has found the only real dignity, the only lasting joy. Come then, Great Spirit, come. Convict the world; and convict my timid soul.

TEMPLE, *READINGS*, 288–89.

NONETHELESS

Screwtape to Wormwood:

Our [Satan's] cause is never more in danger than when a human, no longer desiring, but still intending, to do our Enemy's will, looks round upon a universe from which every trace of [God] seems to have vanished, and asks why he has been forsaken, and still obeys.

LEWIS, *THE SCREWTAPE LETTERS*, 39.

OUR WORSHIP

We can worship God but three ways, we have but three things to worship Him [with:] 1. The soul He hath inspired; 2. the body He hath ordained us; 3. and the worldly goods He hath vouchsafed to bless us [with]. We do worship Him with all, seeing there is but one reason for all.

If He breathed into us our soul, but framed not our body, but some other did that, neither bow your knee nor uncover your head, but keep on your hats, and sit even as you do hardly. But if He hath framed that body of yours and every member of it, let Him have the honour both of head and knee, and every member else.

Again, if it be not He That gave us our worldly goods but somebody else, what He gave not, that withhold from Him and spare not. But if all come from Him, [then] . . . He [is] . . . to be worshipped with all. . . .

ANDREWES, *SEVENTEEN SERMONS*, 258.

DAILY OBLATION OF OURSELVES

Yes, what you want is just what we all want, not merely to touch now and then for a moment in feeling the love of God, but "to be rooted and grounded in love" [Eph 3:17]. So that each day we start from love, as the tree grows from its living root, and go, not to our work and play merely, but to God in our work and play—from love to love.

But we are not to expect sensible manifestations and consolations of the love of God, but to ground ourselves in God Himself, by faith, not in any mere feeling of His goodness and beauty. And if we offer ourselves to God in Christ in the morning, and go on straight with our faces towards Jerusalem, we are not to be afraid, as if the whole day was displeasing to God, because in the stress of the day's duties our feeble memory could not keep God always before it. The intention of the day is the reality, but we must renew it consciously as often as we can recollect ourselves in the course of the day. It is physically impossible to think of two things at the same time probably; and if the moment's work takes all our thought it is probably impossible to do better. If our will is directed towards God, if we have stirred up the gift of God that is in us by our morning recollection, then when there is a break in occupations which need all our attention we can look up again and remember that we are not a wheel in an earthly machine, but that we have a secret link with God in heaven, and that Christ on the throne is also in our heart, and that we carry Him into the mechanical occupations of the day. But that implies that we bring perfection, and graciousness, and joy of gratitude, and patience, and other good dispositions, into the commonplace things we are doing.

CONGREVE, SPIRITUAL LETTERS, 117–18.

LONGING FOR PERFECTION

How is it, then, that every man seems born with this one thing, a longing for perfection; and yet this one thing, perfection, seems to be almost the only thing man does not by any chance succeed in attaining? It seems as if the law of his nature was that he must long for perfection, but it is absolutely impossible he should ever become perfect. The answer to the difficulty is to admit that man is created for perfection, and then to learn that perfection is not in himself or in any creature, or natural method, or system, but that man's perfection is God Himself.

Man was created for God: that explains his hunger and restlessness after God. It explains also his disappointment with himself and every creature. He was not created for any good less than the Infinite. It is no wonder that he fails to find perfection in any creature; but in God he does find it. And this is the only solution also practically. It is only a life that aims at God that will persevere under all circumstances to the end in trying to do better, to rise.

In youth our visions of perfection start us in various enterprises; in middle life the failure to attain what we eagerly sought is apt to chill and deaden hope and effort. Ideals begin to fall like leaves with the first frost, when we begin to grow old. But sometimes you will see a tree that keeps every leaf green right through the winter. A life that never loses the ideal: this will be a life that never loses God out of the heart. God is that man's ideal; and look also, "his leaf doth not wither" [Ps 1:4].

It seems that there is no created thing, nor person, perfect in itself. Any created thing's perfection is its capacity of fitting into God's plan. A man's perfection is his relation to God, his faculty of receiving God, responding to God, growing like God. This is the meaning of "Thou shalt love the Lord thy God with all thy heart, mind, soul, etc." [Matt 22:37–40].

CONGREVE, SPIRITUAL LETTERS, 60–61.

PERCEPTIVENESS

I had five aunts who lived together in a Hampstead house known to their nephews and nieces as the Aunt-Heap. They were extremely charitable, and never was there a household of people who so consistently bought cabbages from bad greengrocers because their wives suffered from varicose veins, or employed slatternly charwomen because their husbands were supposed to be reclaimed drunkards. Their numerous fringe of casual employees were known by us collectively as the Old Frauds. One object of their charity was an indigent cousin of some kind who was bedridden. If you visited her you would sooner or later—and a good deal sooner than later—hear her tale of woe. A doctor had recommended the amputation of her leg at the knee and promised to set her upright on a wooden peg. "But," said cousin Harriet, "that very night the Holy Ghost said to me, 'Miss Barker, don't you have it off.'" With the result that she was useless to herself, and a care to others, for the remaining forty years of her life. No doubt an edifying conclusion.

We will now get on the time machine and come some forty years nearer to the present day. A young woman joined an enthusiastic religious group which ran like wildfire round the world in the twenties and thirties. In the solvent atmosphere of a shared emotion she fell in love with a man formerly of bad life whom the group had converted. But just as the wedding began to look like practical politics she was seized with terrible misgivings. Did the man genuinely love her and would it last? She made the mistake of sharing her anxiety with the group, with which, indeed, she was taught to share all things. Theirs was a meeting of communal quiet. They laid it before the Lord and they waited for guidance. The leader uttered the oracle; and it was the current saying in the group, that the leader's guidance was always right. The spirit declared that the marriage was to go forward. The girl's fears were groundless. It was a marriage in the Lord, it would consecrate their union with the fellowship and keep them steadfast in the Lord's work. Very edifying; but the husband quickly relapsed into his evil life, cursed the Christian group with all his heart, brought his mistresses into his house, and drove out his two children and his wife. The woman, being brave and steadfast, worked and brought up her children. So the human race got two recruits out of the mess, for it is God's way to bring his good out of our evil. I find it hard to believe, however, that the evil was the intention of his holy will in the first place.

The two cases I've narrated to you are both true fact, and the comparison between them is instructive. Old cousin Harriet followed her heart: the young woman went against hers. What hit cousin Harriet with the force of divine authority was something which came rushing up from the bottom of her mind, and I could put a name to it—so could you—it was animal fear, the fear of the surgeon's knife. What overbore the unlucky young bride was group support for the leader's ideas; and his ideas did not come so much from the heart, as from the head. The reason why the group held that Dick's guidance was always right was that he had an uncanny skill in planning an evangelistic campaign, so as to obtain visible success in the short run. And so, I suppose, he was doing in the case of this unfortunate engagement of marriage. He was, as was habitual with him, seeing it as part of his group tactics. Marriages within the group tended to hold the group together; and especially to tie in a man of popular gifts, a potentially useful agent of propaganda who was, however, dangerously unstable. So he sacrificed the individual to the collective plan, like any communist.

So, in the one case the heart seized control, in the other the head. What, then, was the matter? We know very well that we've got to listen to our heart, and also to our head; there's no folly in attending to either. The common error in the two cases was simply a mistaken belief in inspiration. You could not argue with cousin Harriet's fear, and what was worse, she couldn't argue with it herself. For she must not resist the Holy Ghost, lest she be found to be fighting against God. And so with Dick's guidance: once it was acclaimed as the voice of God, it was irresistible. The young lady should have been free to say: I see the force of Dick's view—it is perfectly true that marriages within the group are helpful to the group and to its evangelistic work, but only if these marriages are sound. Now as to whether this marriage in particular is sound, neither Dick nor any other member of the group is so well placed for judging as

I am. It is I who feel the quality of the man's attitude to me and it fills me with a misgiving which no amount of argument can quiet or dispel.

The trouble about an indiscreet belief in inspiration is that it smothers reason. A man who declares "This is what the Spirit directs" is not required to give a reason; surely God does not argue his cases. But I say to you, always suspect claims to inspired guidance which bypass reasoned argument. There are not fewer reasons for what God ordains than for other things; there are more, far more. There are all the reasons in the world, if we can but find them. For is not he wise?

If I were sitting where you sit, and hearing the preacher produce these old skeletons out of the family cupboard, I think that I should be saying something like this. "The man is talking common sense and flat worldly wisdom, and I wouldn't want to dispute it on that level. Only what he is saying amounts to this—that the Christian Gospel isn't true, but quite false. For the Gospel promises us the Holy Spirit to guide us; whereas the preacher says that no belief can be more dangerous than the belief that we have the guidance of the Spirit." If, in fact, any of you are sharing any such protest as that, I agree that it's a perfectly fair challenge and as such I propose to take it up.

Is the Christian inspired? Yes, he is indeed. Just as inspired as he is Christian, and just as Christian as he is inspired. Are we not told that the Spirit is Christ's other self and that the Spirit in us is the very overflow of Christ's divine life? And, as St. Paul says, putting it negatively, those that are not led by the Spirit of Christ are none of his, that is, they are not Christians at all. Only *how* does the Spirit of Christ shape our spirits? I am going, in answer, to give you a very dull word, a word which has no poetic colour or emotional aura—the word is, *attitude.* The Christian who seeks in prayer and sacrament the company of Christ, who puts himself into the acts and concerns of Christ, is drawn quite without consciousness, perhaps, into the attitudes of Christ. And Christ's attitude is a two-sided relationship: to his divine Father, and to his human brothers. The so-called Christian virtues are attitudes—Christ's attitudes passing over into us, to become ours. Attitudes, for example, of faith, of hope, of love. These attitudes, so far as we Christians share them, are simply Christlike, simply divine, and no inspiration we could possibly receive could be higher or diviner than this. There is nothing better, in this life, that God could give us.

The attitudes are the basic things, the immediate form of the divine life in us. But then, of course, they carry with them many particular illuminations. The mind governed by Christ's faith, Christ's hope, Christ's love, is the mind that sees straight, and so the convert cries with the blind man healed in the Gospel story: "I was blind: and now I see!" Of course conversion to Christ brings spiritual perceptiveness: for it teaches us to look through the eyes of God!

Between getting one's spiritual eyes, and claiming oracular inspirations, the difference is wide. Oracular assurances are a *substitute* for intellectual sight, whereas what we are talking about is a clearing of intellectual sight. A good pair of spectacles is not a substitute for the use of one's eyes. When I have the advantage of spectacles, I do not say, "My spectacles tell me so-and-so," but, "I see such-and-such a state of affairs." My spectacles do not inform me, they make my sense perfect, so that the visible world may inform me. The Christian mind quickened by faith, hope and love is simply capable of a greater perceptiveness. Heaven help the Christian whose prayers do not make him quicker of eye to appreciate another's need, and to hear the call of duty as it arises in every circumstance of life! The Christian whose prayers make him more shut up in himself, less open to the glory of the world or to the image of God in his fellows, what sort of a Christian is he? And to what can he be praying? Surely to wood or stone, and not to the living God, the Father of our Lord Jesus Christ.

We say in the Creed, I believe in the Holy Ghost, the lifegiver, who spoke through the prophets. The two functions are one. How did he speak through the prophets? How else than by making them all alive? And when they were alive, then they were alive to what surrounded them, and alive to what God was doing and declaring in their days, and so what they saw they could not but speak.

Well, this is very fine, and if God did no more for us than make us divinely alive to himself and to one another, we might think he had done all we would dare to ask. But does not he do more? Does he not (for all I may say) give his servants special inspiration, showing them things about their call or their destiny which they could never gather from looking round on the world, never mind with how clear or enlightened eyes? Well, yes, he does. I will fish another rag out of my family dustbin for you—a very commonplace example. There was my little old aunt Ellen. She did not join the Aunt-Heap until long after cousin

Harriet's time—not until she was old. Till then she had somewhere else to be, and something else to do. She was the tiniest creature—as small as a mouse, and as timid. In her girlhood she fainted at every sight of blood. But steadily through her teens the conviction grew in her that Christ would have her go to India as a missionary doctor. Not that there were any missionary doctors of her sex then; the medical schools only opened to women in the year she was ready to enter. So she went—and I will not enlarge on the story of her life. I will merely say that if we can be voted into Paradise by the voices of the poor, my little aunt will have had an easy passage. But all that's irrelevant. I have only to speak now of her resolution, or conviction about her calling, slowing maturing in patience and fidelity, with no excitement, no tension, no oracles from the skies, but a growing sense of what God meant to make of her, and through her. And so, perhaps, God will give you assurance of the calling he has for you; and this, I say, is a manner of inspiration which goes somewhat beyond the mere sharpening of our eyes to see what is around us.

Just now I gave you a word: attitude. And now I will give you another—depth. The sharing of the Lord's attitude of heart and mind through prayer is not just Yes or No—you either share it or you don't—it's a matter of depth. We can enter deeply, or shallowly, into the divine-human life of Christ.

FARRER, *THE END OF MAN*, 62–66.

THE BLESSING OF FREEDOM

The first great blessing which God gives us, and of which evil hides the real meaning, offering us a counterfeit, is what we call Freedom. God's will for us is that we should live, with a life that is, in some mysterious sense, our own. This really means that we have the power of making God's life our own, and entering more and more fully into communion and conscious unity with Him. In Him we live and move and have our being, so far as we really live at all; and true freedom is the power to make His life our own, the power to express through our many-sided complex nature, His Beauty and Goodness and Truth. But there is a false freedom, the possibility of which is apparently inherent in, and part of, the gift of life itself; and this false freedom is the attempt to live apart from, and independent of, God; the power to live a life which is *absolutely* our own. It is an entirely false life which is really death, and the sense of freedom which it gives is not really freedom, but slavery. . . . [T]here is no freedom apart from union with God. Freedom is not independence of, but conscious unity with[,] eternal Love.

STUDDERT KENNEDY, *THE WICKET GATE*, 139–40.

VICTORY

It is most needful to recollect that victory over death is a *gift*. I do not mean merely that the final victory over the grave is a gift. That too we may often forget. We may believe that we shall achieve our immortal happiness by some splendid exertions or faith of ours. We may think that is to be won by strife with the Divine Will, not by trust in it and submission to it. And we shall easily fall into this mistake if we do not look upon every preparatory victory of life over death as a gift of God. Each morning that we wake out of sleep, each power that we are able to exert over brute matter, each energy of the body, each return of health after sickness, each hard discovery, each power which the will exerts over the inclinations of our own flesh, each act of just government over other men, each influence we are able to put forth for making other men more wise or more free ... [each of these] we must accept as the fruit and manifestation of His Will, as the pledge and foretaste of a final victory. Believe it to be so, young man, rejoicing in the days of thy youth, in the fulness and freshness of life; believe it to be so, weary pilgrim, struggling under the load of daily and increasing pain; God in each case is testifying, if thou wilt understand the testimony, that life in thee is stronger than death, that life in thee shall overcome death. Therefore give up thy life to Him, that He may use it as He knows best. Let Him have thy vigour, to turn it against the foes of thy country and of men. Let Him have thy feebleness, that His Fatherly love and sympathy, and the obedience that He wrought out in Christ by suffering, may shine forth in thee. Be sure that He has most various methods of manifesting the power of His Son's Resurrection here; but that, if thou trustest in Him, and dost not faint, the end will be the same; all shall share alike in the victory.

MAURICE, *LESSONS OF HOPE*, 99–101.

16

Nightfall

NOTHINGNESS

Screwtape to Wormwood:

You can make [the patient] waste his time not only in conversation he
enjoys with people whom he likes but also in conversations with those
he cares nothing about on subjects that bore him. You can make him do
nothing at all for long periods. You can keep him up late at night, not
roistering, but staring at a dead fire in a cold room. All the healthy and
outgoing activities which we [demons] want him to avoid can be inhib-
ited and *nothing* given in return, so that at last he may say, as one of my
own patients said on his arrival down here, "I now see that I spent most
of my life in doing *neither* what I ought *nor* what I liked." The Christians
describe the Enemy [God] as one "without whom Nothing is strong."
And Nothing is very strong: strong enough to steal away a man's best
years not in sweet sins but in a dreary flickering of the mind over it
knows not what and knows not why, in the gratification of curiosities so
feeble that the man is only half aware of them, in drumming of fingers
and kicking of heels, in whistling tunes that he does not like, or in the
long, dim labyrinth of reveries that have not even lust or ambition to
give them a relish, but which, once chance association has started them,
the creature is too weak and fuddled to shake off.

LEWIS, THE SCREWTAPE LETTERS, 55–56.

NIGHT COMETH

St. John [1:5] says that Christ is a light in the darkness of this world, a
light which the darkness never overtook—not, I think, never *compre-*

hended, as our old version has it: that is not the point in this place. In a sense, Christ was as much overtaken as any of us, by nightfall and the striking hour. Very often, we must suppose, since he was the type of that good Samaritan, who turned aside from his scheduled journeys to heed the cry of need. Darkness overtook him, he fell short of his inn, and camped by the wayside. And yet, it did not *overtake* him, as an alien thing: for he was himself, says St. John, the Word by whom the world was made, and through whom light and darkness were both appointed. He was no more *overtaken* by the darkness, than I am *overtaken* by the words I freely speak. His earthly mission, his charitable action, were one with the cycles of the sun and moon; they all went together to compose the single but manifold purpose of God. He did not fret at the passage of time, it did not accuse him of negligence, nor did it mock him for his impotence. He had taught, he had healed, he had journeyed, he had prayed as the time allowed. That his planned journey should fail, all this was carried in the higher plan by which, human choice and heavenly providence concurring, he moved forward to the redemption of mankind, and the marriage of heaven with earth. He never watched time running through his fingers: when he still had more than thirty years in hand, he spent them at a single throw, and bought the pearl of infinite price. You can say that, in the end, he embraced darkness: he never let it overtake him.

. . . [W]hen [my father] came to the end of his life, he would lament how little he had made of it. And so we are all likely to feel. Time accuses us, time, and those awful words, "We have left undone what we ought to have done"—for God knows what that is. And when we are most triumphant in the sense of having overtaken time, and imposed our achievement on the day, we may have most cause to rue, in our supposed success, the failure to have done the only thing that would have been truly worth while.

If we have to suppose that any souls are condemned to everlasting misery, surely a striking clock will not be left out of the equipment of their prison; the sound of time relentlessly passing, and never occupied to the hearer's content. A life on earth continually overtaken by time, and by remorse, is a pattern of damnation: but if we suffer such a hell on earth, it is only for lack of taking hold upon the redemption so freely offered to us. The Light, which darkness overtaketh not, has shined on our heads: he who commits his soul to Christ is one with the will which made both night and day. He puts himself into the hands of Christ, to live in his will. He will not be perfect, and so he will have many repentances for time misspent; but he will be humble and believing, therefore he will feel no remorse. He will say: I missed this or that call from a fellow-being, I followed my pride, or my pleasure, I did not do as you, my Lord, would have done. But you have let me fall into these errors to show me my heart, and you, in your mercy, will use them for my discipline, and turn them to account in the designs of your loving kindness. You have undertaken my life, and you will bring it to good. While we are yours, we shall never be overtaken by darkness; work out in us the purpose of your perfect will and bring us to that day, which will marry us to joy, and ring every peal in all the city of heaven.

FARRER, *A CELEBRATION OF FAITH*, 190–92.

RESISTING THE CURRENT

It is a sickly age of infidelity, which has not only deprived us of religion, but of common sense, and of the common faculty of thinking. A foolish generation: It is a certain sign of a sound and steady virtue and judgment, not to be carried along with the current of libertinism and infidelity. Let us make this wise choice, to be happy with the few, rather than to go to hell with the crowd.

WILSON, *MAXIMS*, 74.

THE EVENING OF LIFE

How surely, and yet how gradually and graciously, the will of God comes to us. Old age and infirmity have come to me so insensibly that I do not know when I began to be old. That is the way of the will of the Eternal Love; it steals upon us like the dawn of day, or like the evening twilight, but either way it brings with it all the love of God. The evening sky is wont to be even more beautiful than the glory of sunrise; and I believe God has trained us by the long discipline of life to see more deeply into the beauty of His will for us in the evening of our life, than we were able to see in our earlier years.

But whether the sweet will of God comes to us like the morning sunrise, or more like the tenderness of the evening glow, it is really like the light of the sun *which never sets*, but remains always glorious in itself, though at any one spot, in appearance, it has its changes from morning to evening. God Himself and all His love is with me here in the twilight of old age, and will be with me if it gets darker still, and even in the dark I can follow by faith and love the course of His glory. If it travels for a few hours out of my sight, it will soon visit me again with the light of a new morning.

CONGREVE, SPIRITUAL LETTERS, 119–20.

THE LAST CHOICE

If I find no home any longer in this world, it is because God has been withdrawing me, my love, my treasures, my remembrances, my hopes, from a world where the frost-wind of death touches every precious thing, where no good can last, but night falls, and only icy solitude and silence remain. This is no home; this is but a lodging for a wayfarer who tarrieth but a day. God is making all things dark and silent round me in order that dim eyes may the better catch His signal light, and dull ear listen for His call. . . . I shall sleep and wake to find that God Himself is my Home, where I shall come to understand myself at last, and all that was never understood before, all that my youth and age meant. . . .

This silence of my life is no emptiness of mere death, but is rather like the hush of a night in spring, when the earth is asleep, but dreaming of the new birth that comes to-morrow. . . .

I seem almost asleep, but my heart is awake, and full of a strange hope. Memory sleeps, action sleeps, thought sleeps, but love is awake. It does not think, or plan, or labour to remember, but it loves; it is withdrawn from the surface of life to the centre, to wait a little while, and take its rest in God, and there also to have its awakening. . . .

My God, I would not die as the unconscious things, the frozen sparrow under the hedge, the dead leaf whirled away before the night wind. While I have mind, memory, feeling, and will in my power, I rise up in Thy Presence to make the last choice of penitent love, and resolve that I will live for Thee, and die for Thee only.

Is not the one good of life to give it to Thee? That hope makes one rich when everything else is gone.

CONGREVE, THE TREASURES OF HOPE, 18–20.

YES AND NO

The way to God, as spiritual teachers of many faiths have declared, is a way of *yes* and of *no*. We learn of him both through what is, and through what is not. God declares himself in the rising sun each morning, and we receive from him the new life of a new day. Yet all the things we see and hear and do during the day fall far short of God. We find God in another way when darkness fails, when we cannot see or hear or do so many things, when life becomes quiet, and we feel the vastness of the night. Precisely in this withdrawal from the innumerable sights and sounds and activities of the day, we can turn to him who is also above and beyond all of his creatures, the Eternal One who cannot be seen by mortal eyes or touched by our fingers of clay.

As with the day so too with the year. The vitality, pleasure, and romance of spring give us each year a new vision of the reality of creation. The blue sky, the green grass, the colors of flowers, and the songs of birds all betoken the loving power and wisdom of God. Yet the God of heaven and earth is infinitely more than can be disclosed by a field of flowers, or a returning flock of red-winged blackbirds. As we learn of God by the resurgence of natural life each spring, so we learn of God also by the withdrawal of such life each fall. God is also present in the bare bough, the cold sky, and the brown and wilted stalks and leaves along the roadside.

All flesh is grass,
    and all its beauty is like the flower of the field.
The grass withers, the flower fades,
    when the breath of the Lord blows upon it;
        surely the people is grass.
The grass withers, the flower fades;
    but the word of our God will stand forever. [Isa 40:6–8]

Both in the coming and the going of natural life, both in its affirmation and its denial, both in its *yes* and its *no,* we learn of the God who is above all times and seasons, the One who is eternal, holy, and true. So to the Christian there is meaning in the fact that sunset is as beautiful as sunrise, and the fall is as beautiful as spring. The scarlet vein in an autumn leaf is a poignant reminder that its sap is akin to our blood. Leaves also return to earth as we do, and plants drop seeds which (like many of our good deeds) will not bear fruit until another season.

PORTER, *A SONG OF CREATION*, 101–2.

17

The Holy City of God

THE VERY JOY OF HEAVEN

As my soule shall not goe towards Heaven, but goe by Heaven to Heaven, to the Heaven of Heavens, So the true joy of a good soule in this world is the very joy of Heaven; and we goe thither, not that being without joy, we might have joy infused into us, but that as Christ sayes, *Our joy might be full,* perfected, sealed with an everlastingnesse; for, as he promises, *That no man shall take our joy from us,* so neither shall Death it selfe take it away, nor so much as interrupt it, or discontinue it, But as in the face of Death, when he layes hold upon me, and in the face of the Devill, when he attempts me, I shall see the face of God, (for, every thing shall be a glasse, to reflect God upon me) so in the agonies of Death, in the anguish of that dissolution, in the sorrowes of that valediction, in the irreversiblenesse of that transmigration, I shall have a joy, which shall no more evaporate, then my soule shall evaporate, A joy, that shall passe up, and put on a more glorious garment above, and be joy superinvested in glory. *Amen.*

DONNE, *DONNE'S SERMONS*, 218–19.

THIS WORLD

As Christians our lot is to be in the world, yet we are not to be of it. We are surrounded by the world, yet in Baptism we renounced it. We are in it as strangers and pilgrims, yet we have much to do with it. Our duties lie in it, we have to deal with it, bear our part in it, use and not abuse it, conquer it. It is our enemy, yet it is to be our servant; the scene of our temptation, yet the witness of our victory. It passes away, yet it is our birthplace for eternity. It draws down to hell, yet our way of using it is to prepare us for heaven.

PUSEY, SELECTIONS, 14.

HEAVENLY PLACES

To what particular place our souls go after death, Scripture does not tell us, and we need not know. To what particular place our souls and bodies go after the resurrection, Scripture tells us not, and we need not know. But this Scripture tells us, and that is enough for us, that they will be in heavenly places, in the presence of Christ and of God. And this Scripture tells us—and indeed our own conscience and reason tell us likewise—that though death may alter our place, it cannot alter our character; though it may alter the circumstances round us, it cannot alter ourselves. If we have been good and pure before death, we shall be good and pure after death. If we have been led and inspired by God's Spirit before death, so shall we be after death. If we have been in heavenly places before death, thinking heavenly thoughts, feeling heavenly feelings, and doing heavenly deeds, then we shall be in heavenly places after death; for we shall have with us the Spirit of God, whose presence is heaven; and as long as we are holy, good, pure, unselfish, just, and merciful, we may be persuaded, with St. Paul, that wheresoever we go, all will be well; for "neither death, nor life, nor angels, nor powers, nor things present, nor things to come, nor height, nor depth, nor any other creature, shall be able separate us from the love of God, which is in Christ Jesus our Lord" [Rom 8:38–39].

KINGSLEY, DISCIPLINE, 100–2.

ANOTHER WORLD

Many a man goes toiling and failing all his life, working at everything else save in the appointed path of conquest. To surrender the will, to humble the pride, to become like a little child; to believe in the unseen; to know that there is another world than that about us, to enter it by Baptism, to live in it by the Holy Communion; to be guided by the voice and hand of an invisible Master; to be drawn nearer and nearer to that blessed Home of which death is only the portal; to see the solemn pageant of the world's great activities go marching by as in a spectacle; to be in it, yet far above it; to despise none of its beauty or goodness or excellence, and yet to have the life hid with Christ in God; above its din and noise, to hear celestial harmonies; in the midst of its hurry and bustle, to be at peace; to care neither for its honors nor its persecutions; sober in prosperity, patient and resigned in adversity, at rest in life, at rest in death, one with Christ for ever—this is the victory that overcometh the world, even our faith!

DeKoven, Sermons, 363–64.

THE SYMMETRY OF LIFE

St. John in his great vision sees the mystic city, "the holy Jerusalem," descending out of heaven from God. It is the picture of glorified humanity, of humanity as it shall be when it is brought to its completeness by being thoroughly filled with God. And one of the glories of the city which he saw was its symmetry. Our cities, our developments and presentations of human life, are partial and one-sided. This city out of heaven was symmetrical. In all its three dimensions it was complete. Neither was sacrificed to the other. "The length and the breadth and the height of it are equal" [Rev 21:16].

No man can say what mysteries of the yet unopened future are hidden in the picture of the mystic city; but if that city represents . . . the glorified humanity, then there is much of it that we can understand already. It declares that the perfect life of man will be perfect on every side. One token of its perfectness will be its symmetry. In each of its three dimensions it will be complete.

So much of the noblest life which the world has seen dissatisfies us with its partialness; so many of the greatest men we see are great only upon certain sides, and have their other sides all shrunken, flat and small, that it may be well for us to dwell upon the picture, which these words suggest, of a humanity rich and full and strong all round, complete on every side, the perfect cube of human life which comes down out of heaven from God.

. . . There are, then, three directions or dimensions of human life to which we may fitly give these three names, Length and Breadth and Height. The Length of a life, in this meaning of it, is . . . not its duration. It is rather the reaching on and out of a man, in the line of activity and thought and self-development, which is indicated and prophesied by the character which is natural within him, by the special ambitions which spring up out of his special powers. It is the push of a life forward to its own personal ends and ambitions. The Breadth of a life, on the other hand, is its outreach laterally. . . . It is the constantly diffusive tendency which is always drawing a man outward into sympathy with other men. And the Height of a life is its reach upward towards God; its sense of childhood; its consciousness of the Divine Life over it with which it tries to live in love, communion, and obedience. These are the three dimensions of a life . . . without the due development of all of which no life becomes complete.

. . . The life which has only length, only intensity of ambition, is narrow. The life that has length and breadth, intense ambition and broad humanity, is thin. It is like a great, flat plain, of which one wearies, and which sooner or later wearies of itself. The life which to its length and breadth adds height, which to its personal ambition and sympathy with man, adds the love and obedience of God, completes itself into the cube of the eternal city and is the life complete.

. . . If we try to gather into shape some picture of what the perfect man of heaven is to be, still we must keep the symmetry of these his three dimensions. It must be that forever before each glorified spirit in the other life there shall be set one goal of peculiar ambition, his goal, after which he is peculiarly to strive, the struggle after which is to make his eternal life to be forever different from every other among all the hosts of heaven. And yet it must be that as each soul strives towards his own attainment he shall be knit forever into closer and closer union with all the other countless souls which are striving after theirs. And the inspiring power of it all, the source of all the energy and all the love, must then be clear beyond all doubt; the ceaseless flood of light forever pouring forth from the self-living God to fill and feed the open lives of His redeemed who live by Him. There is the symmetry of manhood perfect. There, in redeemed and glorified human nature, is the true heavenly Jerusalem.

I hope that we are all striving and praying now that we may come to some such symmetrical completeness. . . . Do not dare to live without some clear intention toward which your living shall be bent. Mean to be something with all your might. Do not add act to act and day to day in perfect thoughtlessness, never asking yourself whither the growing line is leading. But at the same time do not dare to be so absorbed in your own life, so wrapped up in listening to the sound of your own hurrying wheels, that all this vast pathetic music, made up of the mingled joy and sorrow of your fellow-men, shall not find out your heart and claim it and make you rejoice to give yourself for them. And yet, all the while, keep the upward windows open. Do not dare to think that a child of God can worthily work out his career or worthily serve God's other children unless he does both in the love and fear of God their Father. Be sure that ambition and charity will both grow mean unless they are both inspired and exalted by religion. Energy, love, and faith, those make the perfect man. And Christ, who is the perfectness of all of them, gives them all three to any young man who, at the very outset of his life, gives up himself to Him.

BROOKS, *THE CANDLE OF THE LORD*, 110–12, 124–26.

THE ESSENCE OF DEITY

Why ever did He Who lived in the Deity in Trinity ever wish to create us at all? Why has God made man? It is such an extraordinary thing! The question is why did He do it? Why ever did the Great God Who with the Blessed Trinity made the world, why did He come down and be born in a stable? . . . And the secret lies in the essence of Deity; because God is revealed to us in His essence as Love. It is not an attribute; it is His essence. God is love, and love always goes out of itself; so leaving His essential glory, He willed to take upon Himself our humanity—Love going out of itself. And mark what love does always: it makes the choice, it chooses, and He chose us. S. Augustine says: "God made man for Himself." Well, He was perfect, why did He want them for Himself? Because of the overflowing of His Sacred Heart. And having chosen us, as love always will, He devoted Himself to us, for devotion is the second course in love, as you all know from the holy love in your hearts. It is devotion. If you love your friend, you will be the devoted friend.

And then the third attribute of love is this: Union which is the crown—So the Master says: "I go to prepare a place for you . . . that where I am, there ye may be also" [John 14:2–3]. He wants us to be in heaven.

. . . We are strangers and pilgrims here on earth, but we look for a better country, a heavenly, and God is not ashamed to be called our God, and has prepared for us a city [see Heb 11:16]. My brethren, don't let the sordid worldliness by which we are surrounded keep you down. We are all of the earth earthy, and lose sight of the Lord of heaven.

STANTON, *LAST SERMONS*, 13–15.

THE GOAL OF HUMAN LIFE

God is the friend of men and women; but because of human creatureliness it is a friendship mingled with awe and dependence. The biblical words "glory" and "glorify" express this relationship. When a person glorifies God, he or she reflects His love and righteousness like a mirror. . . . Men and women whom we call saints have been marked by a growing reflection of the divine character, mingled with awe, penitence and humility.

Since men and women are made in the divine image, and the love of God for each and every member of the human race is infinite, the goal is heaven, which is the perfect fellowship of God's human creatures with Him in glory. In heaven God's creatures perfectly reflect His goodness in their selfless service of Him and of one another; and they enjoy the vision of Him, and the inexhaustible adventure of knowing, serving and seeing one whose goodness and beauty are perfect. Heaven is eternal, for God is eternal; and it is the fulfilment of the meaning of human life as created in the divine image, and of God's infinite love for each and for all. Thus heaven gives perspective to the present existence of men and women, and human life in this world is but a brief prelude to the goal for which they were created.

RAMSEY, *GLORY DESCENDING*, 133.

SEEING THE HOLY CITY

Not long ago a minister who had been sent to visit the mission stations of his church in Asia was on his homeward journey. The plane in which he was flying came westward across the deserts to Damascus, then turned southward along the Mediterranean shore. He had been eager above everything to get to Jerusalem, but the pressure of time made that impossible. Now he would not even see it. In the plane, though, as a fellow passenger, was a young aviator who knew every mile of the route over which they were flying. When he understood the eagerness of the minister to see the Holy City, he told him there was a point at which it was sometimes possible to get a far view of it through a gap in the Judaean hills. As they approached this point, they watched with intense concentration for the one moment of their opportunity. The plane swept on, the rampart of the hills flowed past them, they were coming opposite the gap—coming to it, going past it—and they had not seen Jerusalem.

"No," said the aviator, "I am sorry. We have lost the chance." And then he added what he meant just as a statement of the simple fact, but which to the man who heard it came with sudden and startling significance like a parable which he would never forget: "If we had been flying a little higher, we should have seen the Holy City."

For Christians, only God can determine when the Holy City of his fulfilled purposes may be attained. But before it can be attained it must be seen. And the seeing of it will depend upon how high the level is on which our imagination and our desire move.

BOWIE, *WHICH WAY AHEAD?*, 144–45.

Biographies

Father Andrew (1869–1946) was born Henry Ernest Hardy. With two friends he founded the Society of the Divine Compassion, a monastic order of the Church of England. He worked among the downtrodden of London's East End for many years, serving as priest-in-charge of St. Philip's, Plaistow. Father Andrew was renowned for his skill in spiritual direction and as a conductor of retreats.

Lancelot Andrewes (1555–1626) was educated at Merchant Taylors' School, London, and Pembroke Hall, Cambridge University, where he was elected a fellow. A gifted scholar and linguist, he was appointed a translator of the Authorized Version of the Bible. His eloquence as a preacher was highly esteemed by King James I, who elevated him successively to the bishoprics of Chichester, Ely, and Winchester.

James Gayle Hurd Barry (1858–1931) attended Wesleyan University and trained for holy orders at Berkeley Divinity School, Middleton, Connecticut. He was a curate and then rector in the diocese of Chicago, and also taught at Western Seminary. He removed to Wisconsin, where he was a canon at the cathedral in Fond du Lac and later dean of Nashotah House Seminary. A popular preacher and retreat conductor, he was rector of the anglo-catholic Church of St. Mary the Virgin, New York City, for nearly twenty years.

Stephen F. Bayne, Jr. (1908–1974) was educated at Amherst College and the General Theological Seminary in New York City, where he was a fellow and tutor. After a brief parochial ministry, he became chaplain at Columbia University and then was elected bishop of Olympia, Washington. His notable work on the family in contemporary society at the Lambeth Conference of 1958 led to his appointment as the first executive officer of the Anglican Communion, a post suited to his interest in developing missionary and ecumenical strategy.

Richard Meux Benson (1824–1915) studied at Christ Church, Oxford. Following his ordination, he was appointed vicar of nearby Cowley. Inspired by John Keble, he founded the Society of St. John the Evangelist, the first Anglican religious community for men. The author of several books on spirituality, Benson was one of the main pioneers in retreats and urban parochial missions.

Walter Russell Bowie (1882–1969) graduated from Harvard University and the Virginia Theological Seminary. He served as rector of St. Paul's Church, Richmond, and then of Grace Church in New York City. Widely admired as a preacher, Bowie was a leading advocate of the Social Gospel and of theological liberalism. He became professor of practical theology at Union Theological Seminary, New York, and afterward professor of homiletics at Virginia Seminary. He was an editor of *The Interpreter's Bible* and a member of the committee that produced the Revised Standard Version of the Bible.

Phillips Brooks (1835–1893) was one of the most influential clergymen of his day, a preeminent "prince of the pulpit." Educated at Harvard and the Virginia Theological Seminary, he served pastorates in Philadelphia before becoming rector of Trinity Church, Boston. A participant in the broad church movement, he advocated theological comprehensiveness. His election as bishop of Massachusetts was contested, but at length confirmed. He is best known for writing the Christmas carol "O Little Town of Bethlehem."

Richard William Church (1815–1890) was educated at Wadham College, Oxford, and elected a fellow of Oriel College. An intimate of Edward Pusey and John Keble, Church was closely allied with the Oxford Movement. He was influential in the founding of the *Guardian*, a weekly Anglican religious newspaper that espoused Tractarian principles; it began in 1846 and ceased publication in 1951. For nearly twenty years Church was dean of St. Paul's Cathedral in London. His book *The Oxford Movement: Twelve Years, 1833–1845* (1891) is considered a masterpiece.

Frederick Donald Coggan (1909–2000), the 101st archbishop of Canterbury (1974–80), was educated at Merchant Taylors' School and St. John's College, Cambridge. He prepared for ordination at Wycliffe Hall, Oxford, and, after a London curacy, became professor of New Testament at Wycliffe Hall, Toronto, and then principal of the London College of Divinity. A leading figure in the evangelical revival movement in the Church of England, he was made bishop of Bradford and appointed archbishop of York before his election to the see of Canterbury.

George Congreve (1835–1918) was educated at Exeter College, Oxford, and Wells Theological College. He was vicar of St. John the Evangelist, Frankby, in Cheshire, before entering the Society of St. John the Evangelist in Cowley. As a monastic for forty-five years, he was much sought after as a preacher, retreat conductor, and confessor.

James DeKoven (1831–1879) was a graduate of Columbia College and the General Theological Seminary, New York City. After moving to Wisconsin, he became professor of church history at Nashotah House Seminary and rector of the Church of St. John Chrysostom in nearby Delafield. He later became warden of Racine College, devoting himself to the cause of Christian education. Esteemed for his learning, holiness of character, and brilliant oratory, he was the leader of the ritualist movement in the Episcopal Church after the Civil War.

Morgan Dix (1827–1908) was educated at Columbia College, New York, and the General Theological Seminary. He began his ordained ministry at St. Mark's Church, Philadelphia, and returned to New York City as an assistant in Trinity Church. He went on to become rector of Trinity, serving in that position for more than forty years. A defender of catholic churchmanship, he wrote many devotional works and promoted religious orders for women.

George Washington Doane (1779–1859), a graduate of Union College, Schenectady, New York, studied at the General Theological Seminary, where he came under the influence of Bishop John Henry Hobart, the leader of the high church party. Less than ten years after becoming a priest, he was consecrated bishop of New Jersey. Doane was a commanding preacher. His episcopate was marked by a vigorous concern for Christian education and missionary work. He was an early defender of the catholic principles of the Oxford Movement.

John Donne (1572–1631) was a member of a Roman Catholic family, but in his youth he professed no religious allegiance and led a profligate life. He later conformed to the Church of England and was persuaded by King James I to take holy orders. He went on to become dean of St. Paul's Cathedral, London, where he preached on all the great festivals. Donne was an outstanding Metaphysical Poet. Neglected for two centuries, his work influenced such twentieth-century poets as T. S. Eliot, W. H. Auden, and W. B. Yeats.

Austin Farrer (1904–1968), the son of a Baptist clergyman, embraced Anglicanism while a student at Balliol College, Oxford, and was deeply influenced in his theology and spirituality by the catholic tradition. He attended Cuddesdon Theological College along with Michael Ramsey, the future archbishop of Canterbury. After a brief curacy, he returned to Oxford, holding posts at St. Edmund Hall and then at Trinity College, ending his days as warden of Keble College.

Thomas Fuller (1608–1661), an Anglican historian, was educated at Queen's College, Cambridge, and held a series of parochial livings. He campaigned with the Royalist forces in the English civil war and briefly served as a royal chaplain. His witty and popular writing style was widely admired. He is best known for his posthumously published *Worthies of England*.

Thomas Gisborne (1758–1846) was a graduate of St. John's College, Cambridge. He turned down an opportunity to pursue a career in politics in order to take up the quiet life of a country squire and parson. He was an intimate friend of William Wilberforce, the parliamentarian and abolitionist, whom he had known at university, and was also friends with Hannah More and most of the eminent Anglican evangelicals.

Charles Gore (1853–1932) was the first principal of Pusey House in Oxford, where he exercised a wide influence over students and younger clergy. He went on to become canon of Westminster Abbey in London, where he gained a reputation as a preacher and biblical scholar. He was appointed successively to the bishoprics of Worcester, Birmingham, and Oxford. A leader in the liberal catholic movement, he was concerned with bringing gospel principles to bear on social problems.

John Henry Hobart (1775–1830) was a leading figure in the revival of the Episcopal Church in the early years of the American republic. Elected bishop of New York, he devoted much of his episcopate to missionary work, especially among the Native Americans. He founded the General Theological Seminary in New York City to reflect his high church principles. Hobart's motto was "Evangelical Truth and Apostolic Order," and this theme marked his preaching and teaching.

Henry Scott Holland (1847–1918) studied at Balliol College, Oxford, and was a senior student at Christ Church. He was named a canon of St. Paul's Cathedral, London, and later became Regius professor of divinity at Oxford. A founder of the Christian Social Union, Holland was keenly concerned with relating Christian teaching to the social and economic problems of human beings.

Samuel Johnson (1709–1784), literary scholar and renowned conversationalist, was a devoted member of the Church of England. He credited his conversion as a young man to reading William Law's *A Serious Call to a Devout and Holy Life*. A high churchman, Johnson was earnest in cultivating his moral and spiritual life. Besides *The Rambler* (1750–52), his best-known works are the *Life of Savage* (1744), *The Vanity of Human Wishes* (1749), the *Dictionary of the English Language* (1755), *Rasselas*, a moral romance (1759), *The Idler* (1761), and *Lives of the Poets* (1779–81).

John Keble (1792–1866) was esteemed as the original source and spirit of the Oxford Movement in England. He was educated at Corpus Christi College, Oxford, and was later made a fellow and tutor of Oriel College. After taking holy orders, he assisted his father in his rural ministry and during this time composed the poems that were published as *The Christian Year*. For nearly thirty years, he was vicar of Hursley, where his spiritual counsel was widely in demand.

Edward King (1829–1910), bishop of Lincoln, in his early ministry was chaplain and then principal of Cuddesdon Theological College. Later he was appointed Regius professor of pastoral theology at Oxford University. In his lifetime, he was esteemed as a saintly man by many both within and outside the Church of England. He was particularly remembered for the pastoral care and spiritual instruction he offered to the clergy.

Charles Kingsley (1819–1875) was educated at King's College, London, and at Magdalene College, Cambridge. For most of his ministry he served as a rector in rural Hampshire, but later held canonries at Chester and Westminster. He was a prominent figure in the Christian Socialist Movement and an early advocate of Darwin's theory of evolution. He was also the author of novels, including *Alton Locke* and *Westward Ho!*, and of a popular children's book, *The Water-Babies*. A critic of Tractarian ideals, Kingsley opposed all forms of asceticism—including monasticism, clerical celibacy, and non-smoking—and became a strong proponent of "muscular Christianity."

William Law (1686–1761) was educated at Emmanuel College, Cambridge, where he became a fellow. He was deprived of his fellowship upon refusal to take the oath of allegiance to George I. He acted for a time as tutor in the household of the Gibbons, the family of the future historian, and then retired to his home in Northamptonshire, where he spent his remaining years in charitable work and in simplicity of living. Few spiritual books have had more influence than Law's *A Serious Call to a Devout and Holy Life*.

Madeleine L'Engle (1918–2007) was especially well known as an author of books for children and adolescents. Her *A Wrinkle in Time* was awarded the Newbery Medal. L'Engle's novels often combine themes of family love, moral responsibility, and religion with elements of science fiction and fantasy. A graduate of Smith College, she taught briefly at St. Hilda's and St. Hugh's School in New York City and later served as librarian at the Cathedral of St. John the Divine.

Clive Staples Lewis (1898–1963) taught English literature for many years at Oxford and Cambridge universities. As a tutor and fellow of Magdalen College, Oxford, he experienced a gradual conversion to the Christian faith. Lewis went on to become a widely acclaimed apologist, presenting his views in a series of radio broadcasts during World War II and in popular works of both fiction and non-fiction. A leading member of the Inklings, an Oxford circle that included Charles Williams and J. R. R. Tolkien, Lewis is perhaps best known today for his *Chronicles of Narnia* and for *The Screwtape Letters*.

John Macquarrie (1919–2007) was educated at the University of Glasgow, where he taught before becoming professor of systematic theology at Union Theological Seminary in New York City. Ordained in the (Presbyterian) Church of Scotland, he converted to Anglicanism and took holy orders while in the United States. He later was named Lady Margaret professor of divinity in the University of Oxford. Strongly influenced by twentieth-century existentialist philosophy, he published numerous books in theology, ethics, and spirituality.

Charles S. Martin (1906–1997) was headmaster of St. Albans School in Washington, D.C., for nearly thirty years, as well as a canon of the Washington National Cathedral. Prior to his service in the nation's capital, Martin, an Episcopal priest, was assistant headmaster of the Episcopal Academy in Philadelphia and rector of St. Paul's Church in Burlington, Vermont. A nationally recognized leader among American school heads, Martin is still remembered with deep affection and respect by generations of St. Albans alumni.

Frederick Denison Maurice (1805–1872), the son of a Unitarian minister, gradually came to accept the Anglican faith. Educated at Oxford University, he was ordained to the priesthood and became a prominent figure in the broad church movement in the Church of England. He was also a leader, with Charles Kingsley, J. M. F. Ludlow, and Thomas Hughes, of the Christian Socialists. Maurice was professor of theology at King's College, London, and later became Knightsbridge professor of moral philosophy in the University of Cambridge. In 1854 his passion for social reform through education led him to start a Working Men's College in London.

Hannah More (1745–1833) was active in the Sunday school movement, and, under the influence of William Wilberforce, she started a chain of schools in the west of England where the poor were taught to read. She also established friendly societies and other charitable organizations for the relief and education of adults. A popular religious writer, she became closely associated in her later years with a group of prominent Anglican evangelicals known as the Clapham Sect.

John B. Phillips (1906–1982) was a graduate of Emmanuel College and Ridley Hall theological college, Cambridge, and an Anglican priest. During World War II he undertook a modern translation of the New Testament to appeal to the youth of his parish. His translation was entitled *The New Testament in Modern English*; this work established his reputation as a popular biblical communicator. Phillips wrote numerous books, mainly in the area of Christian apologetics.

Harry Boone Porter, Jr. (1923–1999), Episcopal priest and liturgical scholar, was one of the chief architects of the 1979 revision of the *Book of Common Prayer.* Educated at Yale University, Berkeley Divinity School, and the University of Oxford, he taught at both Nashotah House and the General Theological Seminary. For thirteen years, Porter edited a weekly Episcopal magazine, *The Living Church.* In his retirement he earned a master's degree in environmental studies from the Yale School of Forestry.

Noble Cilley Powell (1891–1968) was born the son of a planter in the Black Belt of Alabama. After studies at the University of Virginia and the Virginia Theological Seminary, he became rector of St. Paul's Memorial Church in Charlottesville, Virginia, and then of Emmanuel Parish in Baltimore. In 1937 he became dean of the Washington National Cathedral and warden of the College of Preachers. He declined several opportunities to become bishop before accepting election in the diocese of Maryland, where he was diocesan from 1943 to 1963. Powell was known for his personal charm, his depth of character, and his careful nurture of clergy.

Edward Bouverie Pusey (1800–1882) was educated at Eton College and at Christ Church, Oxford, and later became a fellow of Oriel College. He was ordained a priest and became Regius professor of Hebrew and canon of Christ Church, holding this office until his death. An early supporter of the Oxford Movement, he emerged as leader of the catholic revival after John Henry Newman left the Anglican Church to become a Roman Catholic. Pusey's preaching, which defended the doctrine of the Real Presence and the practice of private confession, drew heavily upon the church fathers and the Christian mystical tradition.

Arthur Michael Ramsey (1904–1988), the 100th archbishop of Canterbury, was reared in a Congregational home and educated at Magdalene College, Cambridge. He studied for holy orders at Cuddesdon Theological College, and, after a brief curacy, became sub-warden of Lincoln Theological College, where he established his reputation as a biblical theologian. He went on to hold the posts of Regius professor of divinity at Cambridge University, bishop of Durham, and archbishop of York before his appointment to the see of Canterbury in 1961. He is remembered for his writing on spirituality and his emphasis on contemplative prayer.

Frederick William Robertson (1816–1853) was incumbent of Trinity Chapel, in the English resort of Brighton. There he was a popular preacher, of widespread influence, particularly with the working classes, who had largely ignored the ministrations of the Established Church. Robertson's sermons exhibited keen spiritual insight and a penetrating awareness of human nature; they became much more widely known when published after his death, and set a new standard in the teaching of homiletics. Robertson's support of the revolutionary ideas of 1848 led to opposition to him which hastened his early death. Early in his ministry he moved from evangelicalism to a broad church theology.

Edwin Sandys (c. 1516–1588) was a graduate of St. John's College, Cambridge, and later became vice-chancellor of the university. An enthusiastic supporter of the English Reformation, he was appointed, successively, to the sees of Worcester, London, and York by Elizabeth I. He was sympathetic to the puritan cause and an ardent opponent of Romanist practices.

Dorothy L. Sayers (1893–1957) completed her studies at Somerville College, Oxford, and was one of the first women to receive a degree from that university. She came to enjoy success first as a mystery novelist (*The Nine Tailors*; *Gaudy Night*) and then as a religious playwright (*The Man Born to Be King*) and Christian apologist (*Creed or Chaos?*). Her major work was an annotated translation of Dante's *Divine Comedy*.

Samuel Seabury (1729–1796) graduated from Yale College and studied for holy orders under his father. He served parishes in New Jersey and New York, and during the Revolution was chaplain to British troops. Afterward he was elected to the episcopate by the clergy in Connecticut and was consecrated in Scotland. Industrious in discharging his episcopal duties, Seabury established the model for the office and work of a bishop in the new Republic.

Robert South (1634–1716) was educated at Westminster School, London, and Christ Church, Oxford. He was secretly ordained during the Commonwealth, and, after the restoration of the monarchy, he held a succession of offices, among them chaplain to Lord Clarendon and to Charles II. He reluctantly took the oath to William and Mary, but declined a bishopric. His learned, witty, and often satirical sermons were popular.

Arthur Henry Stanton (1839–1913) graduated from Trinity College, Oxford, and attended Cuddesdon Theological College. He accepted appointment as a curate in the new parish of St. Alban's, Holborn, in London, and remained in this post for over fifty years. A popular preacher, he had a devoted following among working men, who affectionately called him "Dad."

Geoffrey Anketell Studdert Kennedy (1883–1929) received a degree in classics and divinity from Trinity College, Dublin. He became a curate in Rugby and then vicar of St. Paul's Church, Worcester, England. During World War I he volunteered as a chaplain and earned the nickname "Woodbine Willie" for giving Woodbine cigarettes along with spiritual aid to the wounded soldiers. He became the most famous padre of the Great War. Studdert Kennedy was an active supporter of the Industrial Christian Fellowship.

Jeremy Taylor (1613–1667) was educated at Gonville and Caius College, Cambridge, of which he was elected a fellow. After his ordination, he came to the notice of Archbishop William Laud, who secured him a fellowship at All Souls, Oxford. During the civil war he was a chaplain to the Royalist army and briefly imprisoned. At the Restoration he became bishop of Down and Connor and vice-chancellor of Dublin University. His devotional writings are representative of the strong practical emphasis in Anglicanism, stressing morality over dogma.

William Temple (1881–1944) was educated at Rugby School and Balliol College, Oxford. He was made a fellow and lecturer in philosophy at Queen's College, Oxford, and, after taking holy orders, became headmaster of Repton School. Interested in social and economic issues, he was made bishop of Manchester, an industrial city in the north of England, and then translated to the see of York before becoming archbishop of Canterbury during World War II. He was an early leader in the ecumenical movement and instrumental in the founding of the World Council of Churches. Temple excelled as a teacher, preacher, and moderator.

Evelyn Underhill (1875–1941), a graduate of King's College, London, underwent a religious conversion that led her to the study of mysticism. Later, under the influence of Friedrich von Hügel, she sought individual spiritual direction and became a communicant of the Church of England. A popular retreat leader and prolific writer, Underhill was largely responsible for awakening the twentieth-century interest in the mystical life. Her two major studies are *Mysticism* (1911) and *Worship* (1936).

Alec Roper Vidler (1899–1991), a historian and theologian, was editor of the journal *Theology* for twenty-five years. Educated at Selwyn College, Cambridge, he studied for holy orders at Wells Theological College. He served in slum parishes before World War II, and afterward he became a canon of St. George's, Windsor, where he trained middle-aged ordinands. Later he was appointed a fellow and dean of King's College, Cambridge.

Harry Abbott Williams (1919–2006) was educated at Trinity College, Cambridge, and trained for holy orders at Cuddesdon Theological College, Oxford. He served two curacies in anglo-catholic parishes before returning to Cambridge to be chaplain at Westcott House Theological College. He was later appointed chaplain and tutor at Trinity College and then dean of chapel. After a nervous breakdown, he came to write movingly of the sacrifice of the cross and the tomb, from which issues the resurrected life. For nearly forty years Williams lived as a monk in the Community of the Resurrection, in Mirfield, Yorkshire.

Thomas Wilson (1663–1755) received an education in medical studies at Trinity College, Dublin, before taking holy orders. After a curacy and a chaplaincy to the Earl of Derby, he was elevated to the see of Sodor and Man. As bishop he sought to foster the spiritual life and pastoral care of his diocese, and was active in church building and in founding public libraries. His devotional writings long commanded a wide readership.

Olive Wyon (1890–1966), an Anglican laywoman, studied theology at King's College, London, and did pastoral work among the students of Cambridge University during World War II. Afterward she was appointed principal of St. Colm's, the Church of Scotland Woman's Missionary College, and became a strong advocate of world peace. She is best known for her translations of the theological works of Emil Brunner and Karl Barth.

Bibliography

Allen, Alexander V. G. *Life and Letters of Phillips Brooks.* New York: E. P. Dutton, 1901.

Andrew, Father. *The Letters of Father Andrew.* Edited by Kathleen E. Burne. London: Mowbray, 1948.

———. *Love's Fulfillment.* Edited by Kathleen E. Burne. London: Mowbray, 1957.

Andrewes, Lancelot. *Ninety-six Sermons.* Vol. 2. Oxford: John Henry Parker, 1841.

———. *Seventeen Sermons on the Nativity.* London: Griffith, Farran, Okeden and Welsh, 1887.

Barry, J. G. H. *The Christian's Day: A Book of Meditations.* New York: Edwin S. Gorham, 1912.

———. *The Invitations of Our Lord.* New York: Edwin S. Gorham, 1918.

———. *Meditations on the Apostles' Creed.* New York: Edwin S. Gorham, 1912.

———. *Meditations on the Office and Work of the Holy Spirit.* Milwaukee: Young Churchman, 1908.

Bayne, Stephen F. *Christian Living.* Greenwich, CT: Seabury, 1957.

———. *Now Is the Accepted Time: Writings and Prayers of Stephen Bayne.* Cincinnati: Forward Movement, 1983.

[Benson, Robert M.] *The Wisdom of the Son of David: An Exposition of the First Nine Chapters of the Book of Proverbs.* London: Hayes, [1860].

Bowie, Walter Russell. *Which Way Ahead?* New York: Harper, 1943.

Brooks, Phillips. *The Candle of the Lord.* New York: E. P. Dutton, 1910.

———. *Sermons for the Principal Festivals and Fasts of the Church Year.* Edited by John Cotton Brooks. New York: E. P. Dutton, 1910.

Brown, Peter. *Augustine of Hippo: A Biography.* Berkeley, CA: University of California Press, 1967.

Browning, Don S. *The Moral Context of Pastoral Care.* Philadelphia: Westminster, 1976.

Church, R. W. *Cathedral and University Sermons.* London: Macmillan, 1893.

Coggan, Donald. *Convictions.* Grand Rapids, MI: Eerdmans, 1975.

———. *The Heart of the Christian Faith.* London: Fount, 1978.

Congreve, George. *Spiritual Letters of Father Congreve.* Edited by W. H. Longridge. London: Mowbray, 1928.

———. *Treasures of Hope for the Evening of Life.* London: Longmans, Green, 1919.

DeKoven, James. *Sermons Preached On Various Occasions.* New York: D. Appleton, 1888.

Dix, Morgan. *Christ at the Door of the Heart.* New York: E. P. Dutton, 1887.

———. *The Sacramental System Considered as the Extension of the Incarnation.* New York: Longmans, Green, 1893.

Doane, George Washington. *The Life and Writings of George Washington Doane, D.D., LL.D. : For Twenty-seven Years Bishop of New Jersey, Containing His Poetical Works,*

Sermons, and Miscellaneous Writings, With a Memoir, By His Son, William Croswell Doane. 4 vols. New York: D. Appleton, 1860–61.

Donne, John. *Donne's Sermons: Selected Passages.* Edited by Logan Pearsall Smith. Oxford: Clarendon Press, 1919.

Farrer, Austin. *Austin Farrer: The Essential Sermons.* Edited by Leslie Houlden. Cambridge, MA: Cowley, 1991.

———. *The Brink of Mystery.* Edited by Charles C. Conti. London: SPCK, 1976.

———. *A Celebration of Faith.* London: Hodder and Stoughton, 1970.

———. *The End of Man.* London: SPCK, 1973.

———. *A Faith of Our Own.* Cleveland, OH: World, 1960.

———. *God Is Not Dead.* New York: Morehouse, 1966.

———. *Love Almighty and Ills Unlimited: An Essay on Providence and Evil.* Garden City, NY: Doubleday, 1961.

Fuller, Thomas. *The Holy State and the Profane State.* London: John Williams, 1642.

Gisborne, Thomas. *Sermons Principally Designed to Illustrate and to Enforce Christian Morality.* London: T. Cadell and W. Davies, 1813.

Gore, Charles. *Christian Moral Principles.* London: Mowbray, 1921.

———. *Why We Christians Believe in Christ: Bishop Gore's Bampton Lectures Shortened for Popular Use.* Edited by T. C. Fry. London: John Murray, 1904.

Hobart, John Henry. *The Posthumous Works of the Late Right Reverend John Henry Hobart, D.D.* Vol. 2. New York: Swords, Stanford, 1832.

Holland, Henry Scott. *Helps to Faith and Practice.* New York: Edwin S. Gorham, 1900.

Johnson, Samuel. *The Rambler.* In *The Works of Samuel Johnson, LL.D.* Vol. 1. New York: Alexander V. Blake, 1846.

Keble, John. *Sermons for the Christian Year.* Vol. 6. London: James Parker, 1878.

———. *Village Sermons on the Baptismal Service.* Oxford: James Parker, 1868.

King, Edward. *Duty and Conscience.* Edited by B. W. Randolph. London: Mowbray, 1911.

———. *Easter Sermons Preached in Lincoln Cathedral.* Edited by B. W. Randolph. London: Mowbray, 1914.

———. *Spiritual Letters of Edward King, D.D.: Late Lord Bishop of Lincoln.* Edited by B. W. Randolph. London: Mowbray, 1910.

Kingsley, Charles. *Discipline, and Other Sermons.* Philadelphia: J. B. Lippincott, 1868.

———. *The Good News of God.* New York: Burt, Hutchinson and Abbey, 1859.

———. *The Works of Charles Kingsley.* Vol. 7. Philadelphia: John D. Morris, 1899.

Law, William. *A Serious Call to a Devout and Holy Life.* Boston: E. and J. Larkin, 1808.

L'Engle, Madeline. "Christmas." *Episcopal Life,* December 1992.

Lewis, C. S. *The Four Loves.* New York: Harcourt, Brace, 1960.

———. *Letters to an American Lady.* Grand Rapids, MI: Eerdmans, 1967.

———. *The Screwtape Letters.* New York: Macmillan, 1961.

Macquarrie, John. *Paths in Spirituality.* New York: Harper, 1972.

———. *Principles of Christian Theology.* New York: Scribner, 1966.

Martin, Charles. *Letters from a Headmaster's Study.* Edited by Louise D. Piazza. Lanham, MD: University Press of America, 1986.

Maurice, Frederick D. *Lessons of Hope: Readings from the Works of F. D. Maurice.* Edited by J. Llewelyn Davies. London: Macmillan, 1889.

More, Hannah. *Christian Morals.* In *The Works of Hannah More.* Vol. 2. New York: Harper, 1848.

———. *Practical Piety.* Burlington, NJ: D. Allinson, 1811.

Neill, Stephen. *Anglicanism.* Baltimore: Penguin, 1965.

Phillips, J. B. *For This Day: 365 Meditations.* Edited by Denis Duncan. Waco, TX: Word, 1974.

———. *The Newborn Christian.* New York: Macmillan, 1978.

Porter, H. Boone. *A Song of Creation.* Cambridge, MA: Cowley; Cincinnati: Forward Movement, 1986.

Powell, Noble Cilley. "The Bishop's Address." *Journal of the One Hundred Seventy-sixth Annual Convention of the Diocese of Maryland.* Baltimore: Diocese of Maryland, 1960.

———. "The Bishop's Address." *Journal of the One Hundred Seventy-seventh Annual Convention of the Diocese of Maryland.* Baltimore: Diocese of Maryland, 1961.

Pusey, Edward Bouverie. *Selections from the Writings of Edward Bouverie Pusey, D.D.* London: Rivingtons, 1883.

———. *Spiritual Letters of Edward Bouverie Pusey.* Edited by J. O. Johnston and W. C. E. Newbolt. London: Longmans, Green, 1898.

Ramsey, Michael. *Glory Descending: Michael Ramsey and His Writings.* Edited by Douglas Dales et al. Grand Rapids, MI: Eerdmans, 2005.

Robertson, Frederick W. *Robertson's Living Thoughts.* Edited by Kerr Boyce Tupper. Chicago: S. C. Griggs, 1881.

———. *Sermons on Religion and Life.* New York: E. P. Dutton, 1906.

Sandys, Edwin. *The Sermons of Edwin Sandys, D.D..* Edited by John Ayre. Cambridge, UK: Cambridge University Press, 1841.

Sayers, Dorothy L. *Creed or Chaos?* New York: Harcourt, Brace, 1949.

Seabury, Samuel. *Discourses on Several Subjects.* Vol. 1. Hudson, NY: William E. Norman, 1815.

South, Robert. *Sermons Preached Upon Several Occasions.* Vol. 1. Oxford: Clarendon, 1823.

Stanton, Arthur. *Faithful Stewardship and Other Sermons.* Edited by E. F. Russell. London: Hodder and Stoughton, 1916.

———. *Father Stanton's Last Sermons in S. Alban's, Holborn.* Edited by E. F. Russell. London: Hodder and Stoughton, 1917.

———. *Father Stanton's Sermon Outlines.* Edited by E. F. Russell. London: Longmans, Green, 1923.

Studdert Kennedy, G. A. *The Wicket Gate.* New York: George H. Doran, [1923].

Taylor, Jeremy. *Holy Living and Dying.* London: Henry G. Bohn, 1858.

Temple, William. *Fellowship with God.* London: Macmillan, 1920.

———. *Readings in St. John's Gospel,* London: Macmillan, 1945.

Underhill, Evelyn. *The Fruits of the Spirit.* London: Longmans, Green, 1965.

———. *The Ways of the Spirit.* Edited by Grace Adolphsen Brame. New York: Crossroad, 1990.

Vidler, Alec R. *Windsor Sermons.* London: SCM, 1963.

Williams, H. A. *The True Wilderness.* Philadelphia: J. B. Lippincott, 1965.

Wilson, Thomas. *Maxims of Piety and Christianity.* Edited by Frederic Relton. New York: Macmillan, 1898.

Wyon, Olive. *Prayer.* London: Fontana, 1962.

About the Editors

David Hein is Professor of Religion and Philosophy at Hood College, in Frederick, Maryland. His previous publications include three books now available from Wipf & Stock Publishers: *Religion and Politics in Maryland on the Eve of the Civil War*, *Noble Powell and the Episcopal Establishment in the Twentieth Century*, and *Geoffrey Fisher: Archbishop of Canterbury, 1945–1961*.

Charles R. Henery is Director of Spiritual Life at St. John's Northwestern Military Academy, in Delafield, Wisconsin. His previous books include *A Speaking Life: The Legacy of John Keble* and *Beyond the Horizon: Frontiers for Mission*.